Flexible Guidance

in the Elementary School:

Tested Techniques for a
Stress-Free Classroom

Elaine Todd Koren

Illustrations by Lori Anne Todd

The Center for Applied Research in Education, Inc.
521 Fifth Ave., New York, N. Y. 10017

© 1974 BY
THE CENTER FOR APPLIED
RESEARCH IN EDUCATION, INC.
NEW YORK

Library of Congress Cataloging in Publication Data

Koren, Elaine Todd.
   Flexible guidance in the elementary school; ...
   242 p.
   Includes bibliographical references.   c1974.
   1. Personnel service in elementary education.
2. Teacher participation in personnel service.
3. Classroom management. I. Title.
LB1027.5.K638   372.1'4'046   73-12201
   ISBN 0-87628-118-8

Printed in the United States of America

8/13/26 - B 9.95

About the Author

Elaine Todd Koren has been a classroom teacher and a guidance counselor in the New York City public schools for seventeen years. During her nine years of teaching, she taught in middle-class, integrated, and ghetto schools. And, in addition to her regular assignment, she acted as editor of a children's school literary magazine and began a special Guidance Through Art Program for disturbed youngsters.

Mrs. Koren has served as a licensed guidance counselor in the Ocean Hill-Brownsville district, a ghetto area of Brooklyn, for the past eight years. For most of this time she has been the sole counselor for 1,400 children in one elementary school. When time has permitted, she has conducted a creative dramatics group with children, workshops for teachers and parents, and an in-service course for elementary teachers in classroom guidance.

Mrs. Koren has been an active contributor to professional publications, including *The Guidance Clinic* and *The American Teacher*.

*to my husband and children
who also sat in classrooms*

About This Book

This handbook is designed to help the classroom teacher develop and maintain a sound emotional climate for children to learn. Its aim is to provide him or her with guidance tools for smoother classroom functioning; it also seeks to give the teacher an insight into the guidance roles of the supervisor and counselor, while providing him or her with guidelines for working with them.

The elementary school is a crucial landmark in the developmental ladder of the youngster. In terms of guidance, the elementary school is often the stepchild, frequently glossed over in favor of its older siblings, the junior and senior high schools. As a result, many elementary schools today lack a full-time counselor or any counseling program. Yet guidance is in its most important phase in this first level of schooling. A child's behavior in the elementary school is often a prophesy of what is to follow in later years. The sixteen-year-old high school dropout has his roots back in the third grade. It was there that he stopped reading because he was too discouraged or too hungry to think, or too emotionally confused to apply himself. The hyperactive child in the high school disturbing others once turned a first-grade class upside down. Problems have their beginnings in the primary grades.

It is important for the school in planning the curriculum to take into account the guidance services for its children. Curriculum and emotional growth are mutually dependent upon one another. They are not exclusive phenomena. Guidance, then, is integrated into the whole of learning because it becomes part of the cement of the school educational structure.

This handbook is designed to meet the needs of teachers in terms of ongoing guidance programs. It is written with an eye toward the workable everyday interrelationships between the teacher, supervisor, guidance personnel, and the children. For schools which have no guidance counselor or quasi-guidance programs, the guidance practices fall solely to the classroom teacher. This handbook is planned to also meet the needs of this type of setting by helping teachers and supervisors formulate techniques of guidance.

This book does not attempt to list all of the theories of guidance practices; these have been adequately covered in textbooks. Rather, it offers practical techniques and information gleaned from years of experience in the elementary classroom and guidance office. The true challenge is to deal with the emergency situations that take place each day in classrooms and with the frustrations of children and teachers; it is to cope calmly and reasonably with the whole spectrum of curriculum and guidance problems besetting a busy school. These classrooms may be urban, rural, or suburban in nature; all reveal the common stumbling blocks encountered by children trying to grow up. The causes of the difficulties of the child of the ghetto and his more affluent brother are quite different in pattern, but the blocks to learning are there just the same. Children's needs have a commonality about them. In all types of schools the teacher still needs warmth, structure, and creativity as part of her equipment. She still has to be attuned to children's needs. The guidance program is a life-saver for teachers, designed to meet these children's needs.

Close acquaintance with new and experienced teachers, supervisors, guidance counselors, and, above all, the children has made this book possible. The children have created their unique patterns in classrooms.

This handbook may in a small way open up future horizons in meeting the developmental needs of our children. Some day all may learn with little difficulty.

Elaine Todd Koren

Acknowledgments

This book grew with the assistance of my colleagues and family. Working closely with teachers as a guidance counselor in a school in the Brownsville ghetto of Brooklyn, I felt their influence and it is reflected in these pages.

I wish to thank my supervisor of guidance, Veronica Mitchell, for her encouragement and advice. My assistant principal, Stella Harman-Gaynor, contributed her guidance approach to supervision in addition to offering many valuable suggestions. I must also thank the other supervisors in my school who good-naturedly suffered through my interrogations, Albert Fox and Leonard Cherlin. I am grateful to Miriam Burstein, teacher trainer, for her observations and recommendations on the needs of teachers. The classroom teachers, Delores Mijas, Linda Saide, and Joanne Mancusi served as models for some of the innovative teachers in the book.

My sincerest thanks go also to Dr. Lawrence Feigenbaum, school principal, writer and book editor, for his helpful comments about sections of the manuscript. I owe a debt of gratitude as well to Joseph Nahem, behavioral therapist at Maimonides Hospital, for time spent with me discussing behavior modification, and I am equally grateful to Dr. Cecilia Pollack, Professor of Education at Lehman College, for her enlightening communication concerning this new approach.

My children, Lori and Michael, contributed their criticisms when they were on home visits from college and medical school respectively; my daughter provided most of the illustrations for the book. My husband had the most difficult task of all, for he lived through the birth pangs with me of producing the manuscript. His love, support and humanitarian point of view proved invaluable.

And lastly my deepest thanks go to the children of the book, who are very much alive in all schools; their originality, exuberance, and revelations of youth are unending.

Table of Contents

Chapter Four -
Working With the Administrator 62

Chapter Five - Working With the Parent 72

Chapter Six - Using Creative Dramatics and
Role-Playing in the Guidance of Children 83

Chapter Seven -
Guiding Children Through Art Experiences 101

Chapter Seven - Guiding Children Through Art Experiences (cont'd)

**Chapter Eight - Developing a
Guidance-Reading Tutorial Program** **121**

**Chapter Nine - Using the Sociogram and
Other Guidance Techniques** **135**

**Chapter Ten -
Working With Classroom Groups** **149**

Chapter Eleven - Dealing With Children With Special Behavioral Problems 163

Chapter Twelve - Guidance in the Ghetto 178

Chapter Thirteen - Guidance Through Creativity 200

Chapter Fourteen - Dealing With Records and Confidentiality 214

You open the door to your school. Like Pandora's box, your professional certificate opens the lid to a host of complexities in changing school management and academic directions. As a teacher you are given the trusteeship of children.

Teaching in a Guidance-Oriented School

You are teachers and your students fill schools. Some children sit on seats bolted to the floor, in front of ancient desks, while others sit on movable furniture in a modern setting. Many of these students are wading through rigid curricula in a teacher-dominated atmosphere, while others are engaged in new informal programs which shift the role of the teacher to that of facilitator of learning.

But modern or aged, if your school is like other schools, it has a variety of children, ranging from the highly gifted to the severely retarded, and punctuated throughout with youngsters with deep-seated emotional problems.

As a teacher you have brought a part of yourself to the classroom, and your ability to synchronize parts of your native talents and what you have learned. How you cope with problems within the classroom depends upon your own interaction with yourself, your students, your colleagues, and the school at large.

You work with a supervisor who provides direction, and may also have a counselor who helps the child cope with a sometimes bewildering world. If you are actively engaged in guidance within your classroom, you are trying to meet your children's emotional needs.

The School Guidance Program

In the words of Philip Jackson, "Our most pressing educational problem is learning to create and maintain a humane environment in our schools."[1] This statement describes what could be the most important aim of the school guidance program. Teachers who have been integrating a relevant and creative curriculum with the fulfilling of children's emotional and academic needs have achieved this aim in full measure.

What Is Guidance?

In a broad sense, guidance deals with children's developmental needs. It seeks to realize the child's full potential as an individual and to develop his inner resources. In guidance, there is a striving by teachers to meet these needs. With the emergence and development of specific techniques practiced by teachers, supervisors and counselors, guidance has become a distinct discipline.

Guidance is not new. The guidance-minded teacher always existed; it's just the techniques that have altered to keep pace with a changing curriculum. If good guidance is an inextricable part of good teaching, then Socrates, in opening up new avenues of thought with the inquiry method, embodied the guidance-minded teacher. When reading Socrates' comparison of his function as a teacher to that of a midwife, who although sterile herself helps others to bring forth children, one is reminded of today's trends in teaching. The teacher who facilitates learning, rather than being a fount of knowledge, places the educational spotlight on the children themselves.

What Is the School Guidance Program?

The school guidance program is not some intangible entity; the focal point is you, the teacher. You are the prime mover of the program in your classroom, utilizing techniques, acquired or improvised, and drawing strengths from outside resources. Who and what are these resources?

Auxiliary Personnel: If the school program has some formal structure, auxiliary personnel such as the guidance counselor, school psychologist or psychiatrist, school nurse, and various community service personnel will augment the classroom teacher.

Resources: Resources such as a guidance library for teachers,

---

[1] Philip W. Jackson, *The Teacher and the Machine* (Pittsburgh, Pa: University of Pittsburgh Press, 1968) p.90.

parents, and children, consisting of pamphlets, soft-covered manuals, brochures, and hard-covered reading materials will be available in a well-organized program. Audio-visual aid materials such as film, records, and tapes should be provided for teachers, parents, and children.

Referrals: If children present special problems, referrals may be made by you through the guidance "ladder of referral" involving the supervisor and guidance personnel, such as the counselor. Here, individual counseling or therapy may be provided by mental health personnel such as school counselors or psychologists.

Guidance Committee: A guidance committee can be formed for those teachers who are interested in the one-to-one relationship with a child. This is a luxury not always possible in the classroom. This committee can be particularly useful in a school with very limited guidance personnel. Administrated and initiated by a supervisor, the committee would comprise teacher-counselors who see referred youngsters on a weekly basis. The committee would also deal with the parents of these children and see school and community personnel relative to assisting the children.

Realistically, however, because of budgetary considerations and teacher contracts, free time allotted by teachers would be voluntary in most cases. Because of pressing classroom duties, many teachers cannot relinquish their time on any consistent basis. This points to the pressing need for additional mental health personnel such as counselors and psychologists in the elementary school.

Integration of Services: When the guidance program is working effectively, teachers, administrators, and counselors are all engaging in a program which actively has directions, values, and recognizes the individuality of children, providing for their differences. This integration of services does something else; it helps to establish the guidance tone for the school, an atmosphere which sweeps into every classroom. And the guidance tone of the school derives much of its impetus from another source, the principal or chief administrator.

Role of the Administrator

Although this book is directed toward the classroom teacher, the influence of the administrator on the guidance program of the school greatly affects the teacher's guidance role. The principal or chief administrator of the school should ideally be responsible for a favorable prevailing guidance tone. Essentially this is true. He gives direction and importance to the school guidance program; in so doing, a guidance climate is established.

The School Personality

Few situations, however, are ideal. The school is a functioning unit in a complex community situation and becomes prey to many diverse pressures. Hopefully, you're the teacher in a school where there is active leadership, participation, and close teacher, administrator, and counselor involvement. The school then becomes vital and dynamic, which strongly influences guidance directions. All function within the exciting hub of an alive building and become fired with some of the enthusiasm. A stranger feels this "awareness" when in the building for any length of time. Similar to the classroom group personality, the school has a collective personality of its own.

An Innovative School

Exploration of new avenues of teaching children to meet academic and emotional needs requires a warm acceptance on the part of the administrator. Creative teaching needs creative programs stressing the individual abilities of the child, programs initiated by a guidance-minded administration.

A Guidance-Reading Tutorial Program: One such program that could be adopted on school lines is the Guidance-Reading Tutorial Program, described in Chapter Eight. This program utilizes children as tutors for other children and is geared toward the instruction of both slow readers and guidance problems. It is these children who are often neglected by remedial reading programs.

Class Meetings: The implementation of "Class Meetings," described by Dr. Glasser in Schools Without Failure and discussed more fully in Chapter Ten, is another such program. In the classroom meetings, "the teacher leads a whole class in a non-judgmental discussion about what is important and relevant to them."[2]

Special Classes: There is a strong need for elementary school administrators to take the initiative in setting up special classes for emotionally disturbed children, and alleviate the classroom teacher. Perhaps pressure may have to be exerted along district or community lines. At present, there are few outside facilities for difficult children and the seriously disturbed are excluded from school, demoted, or just permitted to flounder. Practical programs along specially structured class lines must somehow be initiated by administrators to deal with children with serious problems.

The Teacher's Guidance Role

As the classroom teacher you are at the center of the total guidance picture. It is you who daily deals with children's needs, frustrations, and stable, sordid or disorganized backgrounds. The auxiliary services such as those offered by the counselor and psychologist help you, but the responsiblity to establish routines, facilitate learning and cope daily with the full spectrum of children's lives and personalities is yours. From the moment the child hangs his coat on a hook in the wardrobe to his departure at three o'clock, he's yours. You are in many cases the only structure the child knows and possibly turns to for direction. In terms of the child, you are the most important guidance person in the school!

Teacher's Approach to Guidance: Aims

You might have scanned booklets which list all the guidance aims of the classroom teacher. They range from knowledge of the personality of each student to providing for individual differences by tailoring the curriculum to the child.

One guide suggests that the teacher use each of the following approaches to guidance:

1. Create an atmosphere in the classroom of warmth and understanding, one in which flexibility and discipline maintain the proper balance.

---

[2] William Glasser, M.D., *Schools Without Failure* (Harper & Row Publishers, New York, 1969), p.122.

2. Offer positive emotional support within the classroom through encouragement, praise and reassurance.
3. Provide opportunities for pupil planning.
4. Provide the necessary outlets for emotional release.
5. Realize that all children have problems of growth and development.[3]

You look at item one in the foregoing list and see it possibly as a superb feat of juggling. What teacher can maintain this balance? You look at item four and wonder if this emotional release is for the teacher or student. And how does one establish an intimate knowledge of children in a class situation? Yet the fact is that within the confines of your chalkboard, four walls and before 32 faces, you really have tried to understand, relate to and teach these children. You may reflect wistfully that cleaning fossils in your prior museum job was a good deal quieter, but the reality of the class before you has changed all that. The children are looking to you for direction, and as the teacher you are there to provide it.

The Teacher and the Total Class

As the classroom teacher, you work in a total group situation. Certainly the nondisruptive child should be reinforced by being the main focus of a teacher's attention. You are the main guidance person for *all* children, the academically performing as well as the nonperforming child; the disruptive as well as the nondisruptive child. But "there's the rub!"

The trick is to keep the behavioral problems on the periphery, and yet incorporate these children into the group.

In severe instances, the behavioral problems of the class may take over the spotlight. When these children are on stage, you may suddenly find yourself threatened in terms of class control. Sometimes you have observed another teacher engaged in a one-to-one sparring match with a child, challenging the child rather than the behavior. The result is a further rift in class control, and a diminishing of the teacher's image.

The problem then is to focus on the strong points of the class and not give undue emphasis to individual unruly behavior, an

---

[3] Adapted from *Guidance of Children in Elementary Schools* by permission of the Board of Education of the City of New York.

emphasis which is particularly unsettling to proper class functioning.

An Integrated Learning Situation

Along the line, then, you know you must help the most disturbed youngster become an integral part of the learning situation. (Of course these children should be given supportive help from the psychological services.) Gifted children, exceptional children of all kinds (from whom there may not be any other provision), underachievers, and the full spectrum of all the problems which beset children attempting to grow up fall under your jurisdiction.

Handling Frustration

If guidance in the classroom is something that you live with daily, so is frustration. Your second-grade youngsters are probably as assorted a crew as a classroom can boast, and they take on highly individualized characteristics as the school year progresses.

For example, Laurie and Jill, who looked so much alike in September, take on remarkably different appearances by Thanksgiving. Laurie is excessively dreamy, while Jill is very quick in her movements and prone to constant chatter and noisy battles with other girls. You know that you will somehow have to reach both children. Other youngsters begin to present varying disruptive patterns in the classroom. It becomes a struggle at times to silence the class in order to be heard.

Children's growing restlessness by Christmas frequently interrupts classroom activities. You throw up your hands guidance-wise and decide to attend a discussion group with the guidance counselor.

There is an intimacy stemming from an involvement in the commonality of teachers' needs. (Somehow we must as educators have insights into our own needs before we can deal with those of the children.) You see that in pooling problems which are strikingly similar, you are no longer working alone.

You have also tapped a guidance resource person, the school counselor.

And Then There's the Counselor

When a counselor first came to her school, she asked two sixth-grade boys, "Do you know what a guidance counselor is?"

"Sure," one boy replied, "That's the one who gives the kids a last chance before they get kicked out of the school!"

"You help alota crazy kids like Harry here, and I ain't crazy, lady, so don't call me again," the other answered.

So much for the perceptions of children. But what is the counselor's role?

Counselor's Work

The guidance counselor performs many functions in relation to children, parents, teachers and the community. The following, however, seems most pertinent to her relationship with the teachers and children:

- She works individually with children like Laurie and conducts group counseling in her office. Referrals from teachers are screened for further therapy.

- She conducts workshops and in-service courses for teachers. At times, she demonstrates guidance techniques in the classroom and helps the teacher tailor the curriculum to the child's needs.

- She leads parent study groups and workshops. She has individual conferences with parents and applies the information acquired in terms of teacher-child learning needs.

- She attends and participates in conferences and meets at health centers concerning children's problems. She makes teachers aware of community resources to be used in assisting children.

Sixty Seconds!

All things that operate within the school system can become potential guidance problems. The following is an illustration of sixty seconds in the counselor's office one hectic afternoon !

A child got her first menses and became hysterical at the sight of the blood which stained her dress. Her teacher optimistically sent her to the guidance office for reassurance and sanitary insulation. At this precise moment two sixth-grade boys, volatile guidance problems, were sent to the counselor because they were found on an exploration expedition in the girls' bathroom; (at the same moment) that a secretary dashed into the guidance office to find the "troublemaker" who ran off with the milk for the coffee break; (at the same moment) that the school psychologist appeared ready to test a child, who was unfortunately absent. The good doctor stood frozen at the door to the guidance office, clutching his psychological equipment, and stared in disbelief at the hectic tableau which was taking place!

On that note, we leave the counselor.

Meeting Guidance Needs

How many children have you enjoyed in your class who were a disaster elsewhere? Has a highly creative child in your class ever been a threat to an unimaginative colleague? What child has sat in your room creating chaos, and you know he would have done better with Miss Harley down the hall? Teachers have often admitted that children might do better elsewhere.

There are children with emotional problems, who have generated problems for their peers, their teachers, and for the school at large. The child with severe emotional difficulties usually finds his way to the guidance office for emotional repair. There may be an indication that there is a need for therapy and special class or school placement (if this exists). But while this therapy is taking place, the teacher must deal with the youngster in the regular class setting! She must learn to deal with him individually in a special program, adapting it to his needs.

The foregoing points out the special guidance needs affecting the classroom teacher:

Need for Mental Health Personnel

Suppose your student requires special therapy and there is no school counselor, social worker, psychologist or school psychiatrist to refer him to. If the teacher is to receive the help she needs with problem children, adequate mental health personnel must augment the classroom elementary school teacher. In many schools where these personnel already exist, the number is inadequate, and there is a definite need for reduction in the ratio of the number of children per worker. Mandatory legislation should be passed by the states determining these ratios. Placing one counselor in a large elementary school, where the need for several exists, is of little value to the teacher. In many schools, pyschologists, because of huge caseloads, are only able to accomplish routine testing, instead of much-needed therapy with children.

Need for Proper Class Placement

There is a need for the correct placement of children at promotion time with respect to emotional as well as academic needs. The counselor and supervisor should consider the placement of children with special needs very carefully.

The highly creative child should be given a creative teacher (refer to Chapter Thirteen).

The very disturbed youngster with problems must be placed with a teacher not solely because she is "strong." Not being allowed to move in class does not provide outlets for the child's nervous energy. The hostile high-strung child who is so contained in a rigid environment is doubly destructive when freed from it. Disturbed youngsters need structured teachers, but also sympathetic ones who provide them with emotional and academic outlets.

Need for Coping Techniques

The problem of the teacher in daily classroom contacts is one of coping techniques.

If you send a child to the counselor for a time (once or twice a week) you must find skills with which to cope with him the balance of the time. When the child returns from a counseling session, you face him with renewed optimism and he returns the compliment by suddenly punching his neighbor in the face. This is done for no apparent reason other than to vent the balance of his retroactive anger. You stare at him, dumbfounded in despair, and are about to abandon the whole mental health approach, resorting solely to authoritarian methods. Yet somehow you will have to develop new coping techniques with which to deal with him, because he is still sitting in your third row of children.

Need for More Individualization

Guidance through increased classroom insights and techniques in dealing with individual children will be a partial answer to your task of coping with children with academic and emotional problems. Increased individualization within the class framework in terms of children's needs and more relevancy in terms of the curriculum are needed.

"To make the school fit the child — instead of making the child fit the school" was said by A.S. Neill in Summerhill.[4] The reverse is the primary fault of much teaching, for example, in ghetto schools and their ensuing crashing cultural conflict between middle-class mores and ghetto values.

A school has classrooms. If teachers, supervisors and counselors are supportive of one another, then what will be created will be a living classroom; it will be relative to the fiber of the children's lives and dynamic in terms of the individuality of each child.

Summary

The teacher's guidance role with children is augmented by the supervisor and guidance counselor. The teacher may work within an overall school guidance program, implementing auxiliary services which supplement the classroom functioning.

The guidance tone of the school is established by the chief administrator, and prevailing school attitudes influence class functioning. The administrator also helps initiate innovative programs designed to meet the child's needs.

The importance of the classroom teacher in her guidance role stems from her daily closeness in working with and meeting the special needs of children. She utilizes any guidance services and techniques available within the school.

The guidance counselor, working with the teacher, deals mainly with children who have severe emotional problems; basically, however, she is responsible for the needs of all children. She provides an important auxiliary guidance service.

There is a need for more mental health personnel, good class placement of the child, coping techniques for teachers and increased individualization of the curriculum as a means of meeting some of the guidance needs of the child.

---

[4] A.S. Neill, *Summerhill* (New York: Hart Publishing Co., 1960), p.4.

Chapter Two

Class 3-3   It is Tuesday.
Dear Miss Harrison,
    I am writing this to tell you that I am not very happy. The
girls in the class always pick on me. The boys sometimes do.
Everyone laffs at me and I always feel bad and want to cry. Miss
Harrison I know that teachers are not the same people as
mommys but if you would love me I wouldent cry. Please. What
about me?
                                       Yours truely,
                                       Amy in row 3. I have a ponytail.

Ways to Recognize
Each Child's Importance

Schools have changed but the Amys are still in the classroom;
their emotional needs are still the same. At least the gospel of the
3R's has mellowed over the years and we now take a closer look at
the child who was repeating by rote a host of irrelevancies. Our
mature teachers look back wistfully to the "good old days" of
their childhood, at classrooms of obedient children and minor
discipline problems. They forget the frequent faceless anonymity
and academic uniformity of those classrooms and the child who
was ridiculed as "different" because he or she questioned,
responding to inner needs.

With changing social and cultural patterns and the resulting
attempts to affect a more vital and relevant curriculum, we
educators grope for new ways to meet each child's needs and
recognize each child's importance in the total class picture. This
presents an ever-growing challenge for the classroom teacher.

What About Me? The Needs of Children

Amy is a third grader, but she asks the question that children of all grades ask, "What about me?" This is because Amy's needs are basic and similar to the needs of all children. What are these needs?

Louis Raths identified eight needs of children, and they are briefly: the need for belonging; the need for achieving; the need for economic security; freedom from excessive fear; the need for love and affection; the need to be free from intense feelings of guilt; the need for self-respect; and the need for being understood.[1]

Of what value is it, then, to the teacher to know these needs of children? Is this just textbook jargon that has been read repeatedly throughout his or her professional training, or is it valid to assume that the teacher in meeting the child's needs has found a potent means for achievement and class management?

About the Third Grader and the Eight-Year-Old

Let's look at the third year, the grade of Amy. Upon closer scrutiny it proves to be flourishing richly in terms of children's needs to be met. This in itself is not unusual. In the past, the guidance committee had struggled with a third year in which problems had come to full flowering and vented themselves in patterns of aggression and open defiance. The third year appears to be a crucial one in terms of children's development. As a counselor I have found this to be so in my own school. Why?

Perhaps the answer is to be found in the needs of the eight-year-old child. One authority states, "At about eight years of age most children begin to unify and to defend their opinions and also to change their point of view upon the presentation of facts. They are also capable of understanding differences between two ideas, of systemizing them and of organizing them according to various attributes or problems."[2] (Of course we are dealing with a

---

[1] Louis E. Raths and Anna Porter Burrell, *Understanding the Problem Child* (Fairfield, N.J.: The Economics Press, 1963), pp.7-19.

[2] Marie A. Mehl, Hubert H. Mills, Harl R. Douglass and Mary-Margaret Scobey, *Teaching in Elementary School* (New York: The Ronald Press Company, 1965), p.33.

norm here and children vary greatly.) There is no doubt that the eight-year-old is questioning, re-evaluating, and thinking, and this can be disconcerting to the classroom teacher who is feeding information to the class. The youngster demands more meaningful rationale for classroom procedures and activities. In his reassessment of information given to him he may be a potential source for class leadership or unfortunately may spell out conflict in the classroom. Too often it is the latter which takes place.

One such class of eight-year-olds is sending out more than its share of distress signals this year. It is class 3-3, the class of Amy.

The Needs of Class 3-3

You are Miss Harrison and the teacher of class 3-3 and this year the task seems overwhelming. You search for reasons for your concern. It's not the first time you've been confronted with a difficult class and you met the challenge. When examining the class composition, you note that the ratio of girls to boys is the same as it has been in the past classes you have taught and the reading levels as scattered. You have the same promising youngsters, the bright stars of the class who may be ready for the fourth-grade readers, and those lagging behind struggling on second-grade readers. Then why does this class loom up this year as a particular problem?

The answer is sitting before you in over thirty-three seats. Children are everywhere! There are just too many of them in the class! With the slashing of the school budget and the loss of a third-grade teacher, seven children have been added to each of the four classes on the grade. You look over the classroom and it seems as though an interminable number of children beset with innumerable difficulties confront you. The school is a racially mixed one and the tense racial problems present academic difficulties of a varied nature. You dream of fifteen in a class, but the reality of the huge group confronts you! All the children clamor for your attention but there's a special urgency...

About Walter

Walter is a gifted child and really belongs in a special class for gifted children which your school does not have. You were bestowed with the dubious honor of having Walter when the classes overflowed, largely because he was a behavior problem. He became your star pupil academically and histrionically. Walter is a continual clown, not unusual because every class has one, but unusual in his special abilities in a game called "provoking the teacher," as in Figure 2-1. In this game Walter is a master. He echoes you, mimics you, shouts out from nowhere, makes strange werewolf noises (left over from an old horror movie on TV), and occasionally stands up and just leers at you with an unearthly expression on his face. You have been informed by his mother, a psychologist herself, and other experts that he's a bit precocious and affected by science fiction experimenting in a laboratory at home. But when he once tried one of his home-made concoctions at the science table at the back of the room, nearly exploding the science corner, your nerves put an end to it. You politely suggested to his mother that he confine his experimentation to his basement. This young man gets to you and he enjoys every minute of it. He watches the blood rise in your cheeks with glee, notices the way you press your lips together in rising anger, and when he feels that he has not gone far enough, he starts a new set of vulpine noises which ultimately travel around the room.

FIGURE 2-1

You look at this budding genius named Walter in the first row and he leers back at you and you remind yourself to keep calm because he is only a child. You are possessed, however, with a strong desire to box his ears and shut him out of the room. You know that eventually you'll have to reach him, for undoubtedly, he is yours 'til June!

About Amy

Amy is the girl in the "third row with the ponytail." When you read her pathetic little note you feel her terrible need to be loved and to belong.

Amy is a victim. Hers is a self-fulfilling prophecy, for in due time, in every classroom, she ultimately gets her neighboring children to point a finger at her. She has a desperate need for self-appraisal and to learn not to care so much. Amy cries frequently, and has difficulty in verbally fighting back, absorbing and internalizing all abuse like a pincushion. She has been referred to the school psychologist and experimentally engaged in a therapy group of children, which proved too stimulating for her.

When you read Amy's pathetic little note your heart went out to her, but have to admit that there are times she annoys you. You long to administer some magic pill of self-assertiveness, but trying to force Amy to fight back only reinforces her defenses and makes her more sensitive.

In speaking to the psychologist and the new counselor in your school about Amy's need, it was suggested that you try to build Amy's strengths through the curriculum. You try to engage her in activities in which she excels. In a class sociogram (see Chapter Nine) she indicated a wish to sit beside a particular girl, and you try a change of seats. A friendship begins to spring up between the pair, reducing Amy's feeling of isolation.

You look at Amy sitting in the third row and think that although Amy's problem may be lifelong, it's only November!

About Robert

Robert is bright but an underachiever. On the surface, Robert seems a bit stubborn, but one soon learns that Robert cannot take thwarting, for when reprimanded, even mildly at times, Robert re-enacts a ritual. He stares at you quietly, goes to the wardrobe closet without permission, takes his coat and calmly walks out of the room. It is useless to attempt to stop him. It is his véry cool behavior which amazes you and the class. The ritual ends when after a few minutes he gets bored in the corridor and makes his re-entry into the classroom. It is a scene which the children know by heart and have come to expect. Children, loving consistency, would be disappointed if the playlet ran differently.

You look at Robert in the last row as he looks back at you with intelligent wide-set eyes and you know that this bright boy could perform better academically. You have the growing feeling that by Easter he will abandon this game of leaving the classroom because he won't be quite so angry, or so insecure. You are working on it!

And Then There's

Suzie: She has the responsibility of getting her younger siblings off to school in the morning so that her mother, who is now without a husband, can work. Suzie generally falls asleep at her desk from exhaustion and you wonder in what teaching manuals you are able to obtain the answer to the problem of meeting with the working mother, a problem compounded by the lack of a husband and small children to be watched!

Deborah: Suzie's buddy in class talks to herself and laughs aloud at her own jokes; she is a child whom others keep away from, except Suzie, because she frequently wets her pants and the odor of urine surrounds her like an aura. Your nostrils flair and you know that Deborah's done it again!

Morning and Afternoon Children: There are several of them like Lucy and Linda. Their learning batteries go dead by noontime, and they are in a state of oblivion by dismissal.

The afternoon children, like Derrek, come in late, take several hours to warm up and reach their full potential by 3:00 P.M. These afternoon children are magnificent in their after-school playyard activities, but rarely in school.

Can You Meet the Children's Needs?

You don't see yourself as the divisive teacher of class 3-3, or one who makes children feel unwanted. Some of the children come from homes with stable relationships, some come from homes that are sordid and disorganized ard highly stultifying to the young. You will have to deal with the worst of this by answering any of their unfulfilled needs. Is it possible to meet these needs in this large class situation? If so, where do you begin to accomplish this?

The answer may lie in motivational activities and sharing of responsibilities. It is in a sharing of the classroom activities through cooperative planning (under the teacher's guidance) that each child's voice will be heard and the majority of the children's needs will be considered as met.

Pupil Planning and Responsibility

What concerns you in relation to your classroom's learning problems is that for the most part the children are poorly motivated. They've come to your classroom, apathetic, sleepy, confused and even hostile. Some are bringing attitudes stemming from family disorientation. Some, like Robert and Walter, need additional planning for individualization and enrichment. Some, like Lucy, Linda and Derrek, need motivational activities. It is your task to miraculously cut through the personal problems of Suzie, Deborah and Amy, problems which handicap and even cripple the children's learning abilities and sustaining of interest. You decide to motivate and encourage them by giving them a share and voice in pupil planning. You have found in the past that when children planned activities themselves, they were more apt to take the responsibility of carrying them out.

Planning: Changing Concepts

The daily plan, part of the morning exercises, is a procedure that you and even your most authoritarian colleagues have commonly adopted. Even in the most teacher-directed classroom, planning the day's activities with the class has become accepted as a desirable practice. But you know that in many classrooms, it ends there at the chalkboard. It becomes a meaningless gesture in cooperative planning. True teacher-pupil planning was not easy to come by for those like yourself, whose orientation ten years ago was toward a teacher-dominated classroom. Then, slowly, through trial and error, your concepts began to change. You saw that when children planned they began to develop direction and inner discipline.

Steps in Planning

In planning activities for the children's involvement, you found that certain stages must be recognized in order for the children to get the maximum benefit from them:

1. The child must really be listened to in order to have his needs and wishes understood.
2. What is planned must be something that the child can really achieve.
3. The child must have familiarity enough with the idea to plan it.
4. The child's sense of success must be reinforced so he understands that he is achieving.

Cooperative Planning

The teacher may plan with the class as a whole or may plan with groups. "They may be groups preparing a record of an experiment, researching a specific topic, or planning a mural, a time line, or other means of organizing information."[3]

The need for belonging is answered when each child has a voice in the classroom. When children set up their own classroom standards for enforcing rules and regulations, the discipline is not forced from an outside authority, but rather from within. The children then begin to develop self-discipline because they have a share and investment in the class and its future.

Self-government is ideal for your third-grade class in conjunction with a unit on government. It might begin at election time in November. Class officers may be chosen and then the class may draw up a constitution. This is all done with the guidance of you, the classroom teacher. The younger child in the third year is only beginning to understand the rudiments of self-government, but the child can begin to understand that he has a part in the establishing of class rules and their enforcement. There should be a general class forum periodically to discuss and evaluate the class government and rules set up. One is reminded of the "General School Meeting"[4] of Summerhill in which each child has one vote. As in

---

[3] Marie A. Mehl, Hubert H. Mills, Harl R. Douglass and Mary-Margaret Scobey, *Teaching in Elementary School* (New York: The Ronald Press Company, 1965) p.138.

[4] A.S. Neill, *Summerhill* (New York: Hart Publishing Co., 1960), p.45.

Summerhill, a chairman will be elected to preside at this class forum, and the chairman will appoint his or her successor for the next meeting. This experiment may be conducted (with guidance by the teacher) as long as wished.

Learning Centers

Within the classroom, learning centers set up in strategic corners of the room should be of constant interest to the restless child. Social studies, science centers, art centers, creative writing centers and a math corner should be supervised by the children themselves by having a child-appointed monitor. Time for participating at the various activities and rules for handling materials should be agreed upon by the children. One of these centers can be presided over by the intellectually active Walter, if that is so designated by the other children. (You may tactfully steer this selection, although caution must be exerted to refrain from interference in child-directed activities. The natural temptation might be to control children's activities.) Interesting reading matter, art materials, science collection, and manipulative materials for mathematics will spark the interest of the children.

Unification Project

In a class such as 3-3, it is beneficial to have a project that will unify the class. A central theme involving the use of clay, for example, can be used to involve all the children. Other interrelated areas such as science and math can be brought into the planning, and a carnival can be held as a culminating activity in which art works may be sold to other classes and money collected may be used to further another goal.

Tutorial Duties

The children of the class who are better readers or math students may become tutors of the slower group in the class and feel the responsibility toward them and to the class as a whole. (See Chapter Eight.)

Individualization

In class 3-3, as in many classes, individualization of assignments is desirable. Each child is encouraged to do as much as he or she is capable of, and at the youngster's own pace. Imaginative materials should be provided for these children by the teacher, supervisor, or the children themselves, to be converted magically into other uses. A collage can be made from the inner workings of an old broken watch; elbow macarone can be pasted on wood or heavy cardboard to make an unusual picture frame. Children should be encouraged to give dramatizations, special reports, do creative writing, and a tremendous range of library reading materials suited to vastly different interests should be available.

In this individualization, the key to class 3-3, the pupils assign tasks to themselves and begin to develop a responsibility and personal commitment to the classroom. The children then become an integral part of the learning experience of the classroom in terms of their own development.

Each Child Is Important After All!

If each child is important, then one cannot be favored over another. When you focus the learning on the nucleus of the class or "norm" or whatever term you have assigned to that precious group that stabilizes the class, each of the "other" children count also. When divisive tactics in the classroom cause exclusion of children from it, fragmentation takes place. The everyday existence of the teacher in the classroom, and the resulting pressures, cause teachers to be subjective toward individual children; however, each child must still be maintained in a feeling of wholeness of the class and thereby be important, contributing his or her uniqueness.

Children locked out in hallways, children ostracized by their peers, and divisive strategies when sanctioned by the teacher serve to rob a child of a sense of belonging to his class and peer group. He becomes unimportant where he should be important.

You know that to single out Lucy and Linda for their slowness makes them become flustered because they're sensitive little girls. You know that you sometimes lose patience with them as they deliberate over every aspect of the work. But to single them out publicly is to divide them from the whole class and diminish their role in it.

In his book, *Teaching in the Ghetto School*, Dr. Trubowitz cites children's feelings very well. These are the reactions of ghetto children, but they pertain to the aspects of all children's sensitivity and feelings of exclusion.

"Some teachers don't have patience. They put a certain tone in their voice, an angry tone. You get nervous and you think you're not catching on quick enough.

She gave people stars that do nice.

She knows how we feel inside. She lets us write about how we feel. She tells us she feels the same things sometimes.

I feel stupid out in the hallway. You don't learn anything out of the room.

When someone's disturbing the class, she don't mention names. She'll say, 'Someone's holding us back.' This is good because other children be talking too."[5]

There are indeed moments that become so troublesome that the children need to be separated from the class and placed into another room. This can be done constructively as a temporary situation rather than as rejection of the child by the teacher. (Of course there are children so emotionally disturbed that they require special school placement.)

You have found it better, for example, to put a child like Walter of the werewolf noises into a work corner to plan a new project before he has yet begun his classroom antics. The antidote to the game of "provoking the teacher" is "anticipating the child." Walter may translate his verbal energies into a project in science involving sound (since Walter is an expert at that) or paint his werewolf at an easel. (Of course your supervisor may not see the humor and genius in this coordination of behavior with art and science.) It is certainly a better tactic than to put Walter out in the hallway to wander and become a roving wolf. Somehow, the class has to remain intact — no small feat with Walter about!

A list of procedures which you might try to follow if you are to meet the child's need for belonging are:

1. Don't ostracize, ridicule, embarrass or humiliate the child in front of the class.
2. Don't call a child odd for giving a divergent response or expressing different ideas.
3. Don't lock a child out of the classroom; in extreme situations have

---

[5] Sidney Trubowitz, *A Handbook for Teaching in the Ghetto School* (Chicago: Quadrangle Books, Inc., 1968), pp.60-65.

your supervisor remove the child to another classroom.
4. Don't have him stand in a corner or behind the door or in a wastepaper basket.
5. Don't isolate him except in extreme situations.

It might also be wise to avoid repeatedly pointing out your "star pupil."

What Do Children Want in School?

Much of the chatter in classrooms in not idle but an expression of children's desires and needs. When we try to silence it, much of it goes unheard by the teacher. Perhaps what the youngsters are saying is in answer to what they feel and want in school.

In an informal questioning in an inner-city school, the question, "What do you want in school?" was asked of two third and two sixth year classes. The following responses were elicited:

From the Third Year

"To be good to the teacher."
"I wish I could go to the fourth grade."
"I would like more friends in school."
"If I were the principal, I would bust Eric in the nose."
"I want to take my teacher with me to the fourth grade."
"Some new friends."
"That everybody is nice."
"I want another teacher — this one is too mean, man."
"A new friend."
"I wish I could get a good report card, not just a little good and my teacher should stop calling my mother cause everytime she do, I get a whuppin'."
"I'm going to buy my teacher a present — a new pen — a blue one — because she had hers stole."
"To be a monitor. She always picks somebody else."
"I would like to be happy and the teacher should like me."
"I would like to read better."
"I would like the teacher to like me even when I get bad."
"The teacher wouldn't yell."
"To get 100 on every paper — then I'll be smart in school."

And for one child, his list summed it all up quite succinctly:

"I want a friend to play with, to read better, a teacher who is nice to me, a pretty teacher and one that don't yell and I am happy!"

From the Sixth Year

From the sixth grade the responses became more encompassing and more sophisticated. One legend from a top sixth grade class read:

"I wish I had a new science teacher, and I would like to have more money, a nicer house, and I would like a lot of things in school changed and better books and have people around me that don't fight."

Signed "The Unknown" — who you
DON'T KNOW! Ha-ha-ha!

And from others:

"I wish I could change the seats of nasty girls around me who hate me!"

"Better teachers who don't holler at everything you do and don't send so many letters home."

"I would like to punch Mr. T. in the face because he is such a mean teacher and he don't listen to us and blames us and you can't ask questions. It's not fair!"

"My friend has green boards that you write on in her school and everything is new and our school is falling apart and the paint is peeling and the doctors say in the papers that you can get lead in you if you eat it."

"I would like less homework."

"I saw cockroaches in school like in my kitchen."

"I want Mr. T. fired out of the school and I think if I were the principal I would throw him out the window!"

"James should change his seat (I hope) because he sure smells!"

"I would like more teachers like my teacher because he listens to everybody's side of it when there's a fight or trouble."

"I would like my teacher to go to Junior High School with me because I might get scared and she'll tell me what to do."

"I hate science because we never can ask anything and have to write all the time. My friend experiments in another school with chemicals."

"I wish people wouldn't use drugs."

"Our teacher says, 'No budget cuts for education and tell it to your mother so she can do something about it'."

"They should have a guard in each classroom to keep it quiet and the guard takes you to the bathroom so you can't do bad things in the bathroom like makin' on the wall and other places."

"They should have a different teacher for every subject 'specially in the sixth grade and it would be more interesting. My friend says they have that in Junior High School."*

Finally, from one idealistic youngster, "I hope the world would get better, the school will get better and everyone will love each other!"

It is interesting to note that when the child wishes "to be good, that everybody be nice, there should be no fights and no yelling from the teacher, as well as reading better and newer schools," these are wishes the teacher has also. What teachers and children want may not be that dissimilar. The child who wants "different subject teachers" had a classroom teacher who, when interviewed, expressed a similar desire for more specialization in the elementary school. It is only in the means for achieving goals for the children that a teacher vs. child relationship sometimes takes place.

In contrasting the responses of the third graders to the sixth-grade youngsters, as would be expected, the younger students appear to be more dependent on their relationships to the instructor. Both groups, however, wanted approval from their peers and teachers. The sixth graders were expectedly broader in their concerns and were certainly more articulate in expressing sympathies and hostilities in their relationships to peers and authority figures. Their preoccupation is with their feelings and schoolwork; they are developing a critical evaluation of class and school routines. They have also a growing awareness of their environment such as in the use of drugs, lead poisoning perils and education budget slashes.

If anything became apparent by this questioning it was that

---

*The child was referring to a program for more departmentalization which was to have begun in the sixth grade in the school. It was to have used the talents of teachers in respective subject areas, and have given the children advanced training in J.H.S. routines. Unfortunately the program could not be initiated.

there is a desperate need for both children and teachers to communicate and listen to one another. The children have the need to be accepted by their peers and teachers, and to be treated fairly by them. The problem of the disliked teacher is not so much one of strictness but of fairness. Children's wants count for something in the shaping of classes and school atmosphere. They influence their attitudes toward work, peers and authority figures, and there is evidence of it here. If there is one conclusive answer to the question, "What do you want in school?" it is definitely, "Acceptance."

Cultivating the Children's Abilities

As a teacher of disadvantaged children in a slum area, and also of youngsters in a middle-class environment, one thing became evident to me. Children have a tremendous untapped potential which frequently lies dormant in many classrooms. The slow readers of the ghetto and slow children in general possess abilities which remain dormant until something opens the door and they begin to blossom. "The Tortoise and the Hare," a rather overworked fable, still holds true in our classrooms.

While writing this I remember Henry, his thin, dark face, huge spectacles and his easel. It was through Henry's painting that I reached this fourth-grade child.

An Easel for Henry

It was during my last year as a teacher in a slum area in Brooklyn that I met Henry Cannon. I remember with what fervor he tackled a drawing paper. It was with the same fervor that he entered my classroom each morning swinging his books madly to the class and shouting, "Shut up you drunkin' bum" randomly to the air.

The class was a rough one, the bottom of the fourth grade; there were thirty hand-picked students, but Henry was the last straw. He could turn a row of movable chairs and desks upside down in approximately 30 seconds. He found devious little ways of tormenting other children; notebooks mysteriously disappeared from desks, pencils were found hidden in the most unlikely places, test papers were torn up, and notebook paper was scribbled on. And through it all sat Henry grinning like the cat from Alice in Wonderland.

Use of Art: Somewhere around Christmas time Henry and I declared a truce! We had found a meeting ground, art! I gave Henry full supervision of an art corner we set up in the back of the room and it became his personal territory. Because he supervised the area, he became very strict about the enforcement of rules when it concerned working regulations for children in the corner.

Henry painted a huge mural of New York City. He painted himself into it as a disproportionately large figure walking down his street. This mural was done on a bulletin board extending the full width of the back of the classroom. He generously allowed others to fill in minute details while he painted other scenes of city streets at his desk. The tenements were all graphic and vivid with color. Once a week he was sent to a special art teacher who visited the school. Henry was making progress and was showing a flair for art.

The *pièce de résistance* for Henry was his easel! It was an old classroom easel which was broken on one side through constant use and abuse. Each day he scrubbed it down, and crudely tried to fix its missing nuts and bolts. Our class had been promised a new easel, but it had never arrived. I suggested to him that if he would promise to do his work, I would give Henry the old easel when the new one arrived. Henry, though, was doubtful about keeping his part of the bargain.

A Way of Reaching Henry: Henry improved and the art proved to be a way of reaching him. It was indeed through art that Henry and I explored the curriculum together. He not only drew the cobblestone streets of New Amsterdam but entered the world of literature and science, for which he avidly developed an appetite. It was the dawn of the space age. Sputnik had been put into orbit a few years before and there was talk in these early sixties of putting a man on the moon. Henry painted flaming spaceships and starry constellations.

At the end of the year, a new easel arrived. Henry had kept his part of the bargain and had earned his easel. My last memory of Henry was one of him struggling down the street with the broken easel which he had tied up with wire.

Interest, Interest, Interest!

Henry's abilities in art were unfortunately not tremendous. I doubt if he is now making a livelihood in this field. But he loved to paint and it was a ledge for him to hold on to. He did not solve his emotional difficulties through this medium; it would be unrealistic to believe this. But it provided him with an emotional outlet and channeled very nervous energies. It provided a means for him to learn other aspects of the curriculum because the truth of the matter was that he was interested. Interest is a fascinating commodity in the classroom because it's the lack of it which particularly hampers the slow learner. He somehow gets lost somewhere along the way. Whatever magic fiber pushes on those who achieve academically seems lacking in the academic underachiever. Interest then becomes replaced with listlessness, enthusiasm with apathy. Sometimes the children resort to daydreaming.

The Teacher's Role

Working within the existing framework of your elementary school it is you, the teacher, who must face the moment of truth each day in the classroom. You must identify and cultivate the abilities of the painfully slow child and develop the abilities of the talented one. It is not a luxury in classroom planning, but a necessity because the survival of the class may depend on it. Boredom turns into classroom disruption. Cultivating the child's abilities will yield rewards in improved academic performances for the slow child, heightened interest and stimulation for the bright one, and certainly fewer disruptions in the classroom.

Children are ultimately diverted by what interests them, good or bad, and it's important to build upon this in the classroom. The important thing is for each child to achieve at something and build up a measure of success.

Summary

Children's needs have been defined as the need for belonging, for achieving, for economic security, for love and affection, freedom from guilt, for self-respect, and for being understood.

It is important for the teacher to meet these needs in order to foster the emotional security of children, enable them to achieve, and reduce classroom disruptions.

The teacher has difficulties in meeting these needs because of obstacles of class size, disruptive children with emotional problems, and children poorly motivated. Dealing with the individual needs of children in such a setting is frequently an overwhelming task for the teacher. Class 3-3 is such an example.

The teacher may try to overcome these hurdles through cooperative planning with children and stimulating projects so that each child feels a responsibility and commitment to the class and is motivated to achieve. This planning may be done by the children participating in the setting up of class standards, learning centers, projects, and the use of the tutorial buddy system. More individualization of assignments may also help to reach each child.

Each child's importance must be recognized in the total class situation. Individual ostracization of children and other divisive means prevent the child from having a feeling of belonging to the class.

An informal survey taken of children of four classes, questioning them about their wants in school, showed evidence in the responses of the needs of children.

One way to recognize the child's importance is to cultivate the youngster's abilities and interests, as shown in the illustration of Henry Cannon. This is particularly true of the slow child and the emotionally disturbed one. The identification and cultivation of the child's abilities and interests serve as a possible key to further learning.

Chapter Three

Mrs. Robbins, guidance counselor

Dear Mrs. Robbins,
　　Help! You must do something about Faye Bagby! I can't wait for the moment she is placed! Please take her for a while because the A.P. just sent her back. Do something fast because the whole class and myself are being driven up a wall!
　　　　　　　　　　　　　Yours desperately,
　　　　　　　　　　　　　Ada Green

Working With the Counselor

The teacher and the counselor, by virtue of the immediacy of the child's problems in the classroom, do not always move in the same direction, although both want the child to learn. The teacher (and administrator) must of necessity be primarily concerned with the urgency of the child's problem, often seeking an instant solution or some palliative technique, while the counselor's (and psychologist's) views are generally longer range. And this is understandably so, for it is the teacher who is truly on the firing line, and the counselor is in the rear guard; the intensity of the child's outbreak has usually subsided by the time the youngster enters the guidance office. Yet there has to be a meeting ground for planning.

There is a need for sensible and constructive individual and group conferences between the teacher and counselor and more counselor involvement in the class situation as a means for opening up communication between the teacher and guidance services.

In these conferences, attitudes, aims and techniques can be explored, reasonable goals and expectations can be developed, and clarification of the teacher-counselor roles in respect to the child effected. Unless this is done there will be a cleavage between teacher, guidance, and administrative services.

A Teacher Turns to a Counselor for Help

When a teacher turns to a counselor for help, what is said in essence is, "I've tried everything, so please show me a way, but do it quickly." This is what Ada Green is pleading for in her letter to the counselor. Because of the kaleidoscopic quality of children's disruptive patterns, misunderstandings in terms of goals might develop between teacher and counselor, and if you look closely you might even find humor.

Ada Green, teacher, has been waiting for Faye Bagby to be placed in a class for the disturbed child, and as can be gleaned from her letter to Mrs. Robbins, is quite impatient for the placement. The following episode developed between the teacher and counselor:

Meeting in School Corridor

Mrs. Green meets Mrs. Robbins. "Did you get my note about Faye?" she asked.

"Most certainly," answered Mrs. Robbins. "It was the fifth one you sent. Have patience! Seriously, have you tried—"

"I've tried everything with her; making her a monitor, giving her individual help, and even letting her do her crazy dance in the talent show. Nothing helps, forget it! I don't see what this guidance is doing!"

Meeting in Lunchroom

"Mrs. Robbins, how long will it be before she's placed? How long? My blood pressure is going up and my arthritis is coming back. My husband told me that I don't have to work."

"Be calm."

"It's easy for you to say, you're out of the classroom! (How did you manage that anyway?) I'm sure that Faye is getting pep pills by that psychiatrist, not tranquilizers. I'll swear to that. Incidentally, what did you do to make Faye change so in class after she returned from the group?"

"I made her the teacher in a role-playing skit. She always speaks of being a teacher."

"She wants to be a teacher? Good night! Well maybe — she might do better than I'd doing right now!"

Meeting in Guidance Office

"Mrs. Robbins, I came to inform you that Faye is now the teacher in my class."

"What do you mean, she is now the teacher?"

"It's all because you planted that brilliant pedagogical idea in her brain and she now makes out lesson plans for the class and tells everyone to line up and be quiet. She even wants to clock out at three o'clock like the other teachers. I saw her snooping around the time cards yesterday. She really believes she is the teacher. I ask you that now famous question, 'How long will it be until she's placed?' "

"Not long" answered Mrs. Robbins.

"I won't hold my breath!"

Final Meeting in Main Office

"You had something to tell me, Mrs. Robbins?"

"Yes, Faye is placed!"

"Placed? Oh! You mean she's going to a special class?"

"Aren't you happy?"

"I don't know."

"Really! You wanted it so badly!"

"If you ask me she's not the one who should be placed. It's another one." said Mrs. Green.

"Who?"

"Steven from last month. He's impossible again! No, not Faye — anyway, since Faye has become a teacher, she has become my colleague. Please place Steve instead!"

This episode is real and has occurred many times in offices, corridors, and lunchrooms in the school. A child disturbs a class's functioning for several successive weeks and then calms down (for a while) and a new youngster may take over the spotlight. Each child who has problems has his own unique repertoire of havoc-producing relationships. The trick of the teacher and counselor is to 'sustain' help for these children in spite of new problems which arise.

It is my experience that teachers come for help from the counselor after a good deal of soul-searching in terms of the child; they rarely do so lightly. The teacher may be basically looking for an answer to one or more of the following:

a. Instant relief for the class problem.
b. An instant miraculous change in the child.
c. Some kind of workable classroom techniques.
d. Moral support to counter a good number of self-doubts as to ability to handle a child.
e. Ability to handle his or her own feelings of anger and frustration when it comes to dealing with the child.

The proper approach is best found in the individual teacher-counselor conferences and in teacher-counselor group discussions.

Informal Teacher-Counselor Conferences

Many teacher-counselor conferences fail! The strategic meeting between the teacher asking for help and the counselor, which generally takes place in the guidance office, is not frequently written about, yet this relationship between you and the counselor is the pivotal point upon which the planning for the child is based. The teacher and counselor often never reach a commonality of goals; they never really work together as a team, and there is a need for clarification of expectations for the child. Often teachers and counselors bring to the conference confusions about one another's functions, and they are undoubtedly colored by a whole spectrum of perceptions about one another as a group. In bringing to light and dealing with some of these feelings and attitudes, the teacher and counselor may achieve a common purpose and understanding.

Attitudes Come to the Meeting

Teachers: Teachers see counselors in varying roles and are often confused about the counselor's function. They also view guidance in general and counselors in particular with varying attitudes, which range from total ignoring of guidance functions to suspicion to acceptance.

In an informal survey, the feelings expressed by teachers in various elementary schools were:

"Guidance doesn't do anything with these kids. At least it takes too long!"

"I was never trained to teach emotionally disturbed children. My license is to teach normal children. I don't feel that I should have to deal with these problems."

"Counselors would be okay if there were fewer cases. It's like applying a band-aid on a gushing wound."

"Frankly, counselors I find are very unsympathetic to teachers. They forget what the classroom is like once they are out of it."

"My counselor has really helped me with my kids. We're a good team. There's a lot of feedback between us."

"Counseling? If the teachers were allowed to give the kid a psychiatric smack on the behind occasionally you wouldn't need guidance!"

"Frankly I mind my own business and don't bother anyone. I handle my own problems — don't bother my supervisor either."

"I like the fact that the counselors are doing more work now with groups of children. I think that this saves time when there are so many children to reach."

"Guidance takes too long. I do my own guidance. Frankly, I think the counselor's real job is to get the "crazies*" out of the school so you can teach."

"We need more counselors in a school like this with so many children. It's all ridiculous because the job is impossible to do!"

"He's helped me with two of my kids, but you have to have patience with the child's progress."

"Our counselor is very helpful and she's very well-liked."

"All the counselor does is drink coffee with Sigmund Freud."

"Guidance would be great with fewer kids to handle."

"What are you, the gestapo?"

Counselors: In spite of the ideally nonjudgmental attributes of the role, counselors, being human, err and form judgments about their colleagues. In speaking to many counselors in informal discussions, there were varied impressions of teachers' attitudes toward children:

"Teaching is a rough job; it's a wonder the teachers make it through the day!"

"Many teachers have little sympathy for the kids."

"It's not true about the teachers in a ghetto school; there are some great teachers in my school and the kids are learning."

---

*"crazies" This is a 'neo-Freudian' term the author picked up in the teachers' lunchroom. (This is not suggested for use with your local psychologist.)

"You can count the teachers who care on the fingers of one hand. Don't quote me because I must sound anti-teacher."

"In my school the teachers have a sympathetic attitude toward children for the most part, but that's because we have a marvelous administration."

"Teachers are very unsympathetic toward counselors!"

"We were teachers ourselves once. Remember? Counselors make me angry when they blame everything on the teacher."

"Teachers want immediate help. They don't realize that we're supposed to help the teacher to help the child, and not just work with the child. The teachers still haven't gotten to the point that they accept the full responsibility for the kids. They think — what's the good of guidance if it doesn't perform a miracle. And then when the miracle doesn't happen, they feel that nobody is out there helping them."

"I think the teachers and counselors are not communicating. The whole direction of counseling should be toward classroom management, working directly with the teacher, and away from the focus of individual counseling. Perhaps, then, there would be closer lines of communication."

"Why don't they put more courses into teacher training aimed toward helping the problem child. The teachers can't deal with these kids, especially in the ghetto."

"The teachers want a quick return for their referral — one-two-three!"

"I see fantastic teachers in my school who really care about the kids."

"What are you writing?"

Meeting and Setting Goals Together

Is there any wonder, then, that there may be a lack of common purpose between teacher and counselor, with such a divergence of opinion toward one another's roles and attitudes? Where are we then? We must establish a meeting ground of the teacher and counselor and find a common denominator, and then set reasonable goals. Of prime importance to both the teacher and counselor is the child's functioning in the classroom, for it is the reason that the teacher has asked for help. Toward this end, both teacher and counselor must build together.

In setting goals for the child, the parties must avoid:

a. Expectation of IMC*.
b. Projecting unrealistic plans for the child.
c. Planting seeds for future misunderstanding.

Realistically, you come to the counselor for relief. Usually the relief sought is immediate. You might think, "If you the counselor cannot change John's behavior in short order so that I can live with him this year, why am I sitting here with you?" As much as you (and the counselor) might want that, you basically know that this miracle is not going to happen, not even if the child is given therapy as much as five times a week!

The correct procedure is for you and the counselor to project a more realistic set of goals and reduce expectation for a miraculous change of behavior. This change is then replaced by a gradual behavior modification, and it is expected that this will be slow!

In turning to a counselor for help and coming to a conference with him or her, you are entitled to find answers to questions you may have. By discussing them, you and the counselor can explore avenues and draw sensible plans for the child's functioning.

Teacher and Counselor Discuss

Some of the questions you might discuss together are:

1. What can we accomplish by our meeting together?
2. How do you see the main problem I'm having with the child?
3. How can the child's disturbances be anticipated?
4. Is there a certain amount of behavior which should be ignored? (See Chapter Eleven.)
5. How can outbursts be reduced when they occur?
6. What technique can I try with the child for a short period of time?
7. How can I handle the rest of the class when the child has outbursts?
8. How will your observation of the child in the classroom help me?
9. What background and anecdotal information should I provide for you?
10. What shall we attempt to do together NOW?

---

*IMC is Instant Miraculous Change!

11. At what point *do I give up?** (The answer to this last question is not readily available to either teachers or counselors.)

A Course for Closer Communication (3 C's)

You, the teacher, have met with the counselor. As a result of questioning and pooling of opinions and wishes for the child's welfare, you have arrived at a list of thirteen points which we will call the 3 c's, or a Course for Closer Communication between the teacher and counselor.

In this list, the needs, expectations and goals for a child have been considered. You and the counselor have had dialogue, now, as to each other's roles, and have opened a line of continuing communication:

1. Clear and sensible short-term and long-range goals for the child must be clearly delineated.
2. The teacher is to provide information as to what has been attempted in her classroom with the child thus far.
3. The teacher is to provide the counselor, at the onset, with pertinent information about the child, including records and subsequent anecdotal information for continual follow-up of the child's performance.
4. The counselor helps the teacher to find coping techniques for emergency situations.
5. The counselor helps the teacher to learn to anticipate and prevent the child's classroom disruptions.
6. The counselor helps the teacher to deal with or modify attitudes toward the child.**
7. If improvement is not made with the child, alternate plans must be substituted or present plans modified.
8. The teacher and counselor periodically evaluate the progress of the child so that improvement or lack of it may be clearly seen.
9. The teacher and counselor have a right to meet and question the other's suggestions and methods in the light of the child's ongoing performance.
10. The counselor should see the child at regular intervals mutually agreed upon by teacher and counselor, or some other type of ongoing therapy should be provided.

---

*The counselor may ultimately suggest to the administrator that a child's teacher be changed. "Child juggling" becomes a painful game. If the child is lucky, he may inadvertently be paired with the right teacher by the third move. If not, he may wander like Ulysses from teacher to teacher and his reputation follows him.

**Attitudes, a highly sensitive subject to deal with, are difficult to modify. The teacher must be a willing participant in seeking this change and help. The counselor should exercise caution here.

11. Regularly scheduled case conferences for the child's evaluation should be held between the teacher, counselor, mental health workers, supervisor of grade and possibly the parent.
12. Frequent meetings are to be held between teacher, counselor and parent to establish close communications between school and home.
13. The teacher may be shown classroom guidance techniques to provide a better setting in the classroom.

Teacher-Counselor Discussion Groups

In Chapter One, if you remember, our teacher went to a discussion group where a mutual pooling and sharing of common problems made the burden a little easier.

Some time ago, a small group of teachers, a psychologist, and myself met voluntarily once a. week on our lunch hour. Our discussion was aimed at the examination of teaching difficulties and ways of handling mutual problems so that the group could benefit from shared experiences. We felt that insights could be gained by group discussion and interaction. We would acquire techniques of dealing with class situations using a guidance approach, and with the strengths and weaknesses of the teacher in a classroom of thirty students.

We were ghetto teachers and our children had needs which were unanswered in a ghetto environment. After many weeks of meeting over the familiar coffee urn and cookies, we pooled resources and found that we were arriving at certain goals:

(a) We had to understand and deal with the frustrations and anxieties of the child who left a disorganized home in the morning where his needs were not met. We had to supply him in school with the only structure which he knew and had difficulty handling. The child became frustrated and released this frustration in the classroom and school. (This subject is discussed in Chapter Twelve.)

(b) What we also had to face were our own frustrations and feelings of anger. Some of the teachers were frightened by this feeling of being less than a teacher when they "lost themselves" in anger. It took a while for teachers to discuss this problem. In many instances, the teachers admitted to having exploded at the class and it was interesting to note that the more the teachers attempted, unsuccessfully, to get through to a class or child, the more anxiety-producing frustration took place.

Facing Feelings

Anger: The teachers recognized that children became angry with the teacher and expressed this anger in disruptive acts in the classroom. One of the problems of the teacher was learning to cope with his own anger in dealing with these outbursts. Dr. Greenberg in *Teaching With Feeling* describes this interplay of emotion between children and teachers. "Some physiological release is necessary to relieve the bodily tension built up during anger. Teachers have ways of attaining this release even in the classroom. For example, banging on desks with fists, slamming books or rulers, tearing up papers, getting up and pacing around the room vigorously, all help some teachers."[1] Dr. Greenberg cautions against any anger release that is damaging to children.

A teacher who faces her own anger helps the children accept it in others without the threat of rejection. "A teacher who gets angry clears the air, and is then able to be warm and affectionate, teaches these children something new about anger."[2]

In the last analysis then, the ability to handle one's angry feelings, both for teacher and child, proves vital in setting the tone of the classroom.

Panic: Another feeling which is no stranger to both the new and inexperienced teacher is panic. There is no way to understand this feeling unless you have taught. Perhaps it's being responsible for so many children that can contribute to this feeling. Some teachers cry when gripped by it, some become terribly distraught wanting to run from the situation, and some fight panic with a sense of humor and all the resources they can muster.

I related my own experience as a fourth-grade teacher in which I took a particularly rambunctious group of children, mostly boys, on an educational trip to the United Nations Building. The boys went to the men's room before we were to leave and forgot to come out! I felt panic rising in me when I

---

[1] Dr. Herbert M. Greenberg, *Teaching with Feeling* (The Macmillan Company, Collier Macmillan Canada Ltd., Toronto Ontario, 1969), p.64.

[2] *Ibid.*, p.68.

realized that I would have to get a load of twenty-five hectic youngsters ready in ten minutes! (A mother who had accompanied me on the trip suddenly disappeared into a gift shop.) For any teacher, the prospect of being stranded in the UN Building with twenty-five charges is akin to a nightmare!

What did I do? It was obvious that modesty prohibited me from entering the Gentlemen's rest room. Panic gave wings to ingenuity and I approached a Chinese delegation walking by in the corridor. I gestured and muttered something to them and they quickly went inside and retrieved fifteen struggling boys by their arms and legs! At the same time, they received a lesson in the current state of American education. When the children were lined up I realized that not one word of English had passed between us, as they tipped their hats and made their way to the council chamber.

One teacher in the group spoke of the panic which comes when a wild fracas develops from a seemingly innocent incident and class groups suddenly begin to take shape and even pile on, one child on top of another; there are battling groups of intermingled arms and legs, and you're not sure if the one on the bottom of the pile is still breathing. Sometimes, the teacher related, you call in your supervisor, particularly if he is strong and can pull the children apart. Sometimes you try to make it alone. The main thing you tell yourself is, "KEEP CALM AND IN COMMAND!" (if possible). Each teacher finds her own way to establish order from chaos as she gains expertise, but it's really a trip she makes alone!

Conclusions of the Discussion Group

Here are some of the conclusions we reached in our noon-hour discussions:

(1) The acute realization came that intense feelings were not easily dealt with, either on the part of the teacher or the child. We also realized that these feelings were quite normal and common to everyone, and didn't really have to be mastered completely. Occasional outbursts from the teacher were to be expected but had to be handled constructively.

(2) We had to have expectations for the child's success as a way of withstanding the daily frustration of dealing with failure.

Our own attitudes definitely affected the performance of the child in the classroom, and he achieved in many cases what was expected of him. We found that the expectation for failure decidedly bred failure in its wake.

(3) Ours was the additional burden of relating to children who came from culturally different environments from our own. (See Chapter Twelve, "Guidance in the Ghetto.")

We were educators dealing principally with the minority child, but when we ended our sessions we realized that there was a universality about our meetings. We could have been talking about any child, in many cases. If anything was brought home to us, it was the recognition of the basic integrity and needs of the child. Unless the ambivalent attitudes of all children were understood, and our own attitudes of frustration were dealt with constructively, we knew that some teachers and some students wouldn't make it; at the end of the year, this was proven when one of our group members who was having increasing difficulties in class management resigned from teaching and went back to law school.

The Case of Class 5-4
(Mrs. Robbins Becomes Involved!)

It was February when Mrs. Lorry took over class 5-4. The teacher, Mrs. Sackman, went on maternity leave and the class she left went into an almost immediate state of chaos. There was some justification for this.

Mrs. Sackman was a strict disciplinarian and ran a "tight ship." She was impersonal, decidedly on the cool side in her relationships with colleagues, and believed in figuratively "sitting on the children," a common pedagogical feat. Children simply didn't play around in class 5-4, and that was that! Humor was not Mrs. Sackman's style and creativity not one of her attributes. Although she was only 26 years of age, she was quite traditional in her approach and believed that children came to school solely to be taught. By all standards, Mrs. Sackman was successful because the class was ostensibly well-controlled. The children marched out correctly like soldiers on quiet lines in the corridors and were very subdued in the assembly, being frequently pointed to as a model class. There was actually only one trouble with Mrs. Sackman's children — they weren't learning too much! Their control, externally effected, was superficial and it was questionable how much self-discipline they were actually developing. But in this particularly hectic city school, where the priority of the day was a semblance of order, this was not recognized as a deficiency. Mrs. Sackman brought to teaching a unique talent; she could control by a look, a gesture, and a wave of her hand, and the children became transfixed. They stopped and froze at what they were doing and awaited her next order. She had trained them well!

And then Mrs. Lorry arrived on the scene and the deluge came! The children first became bewildered with this substitute teacher, for consistency went out the window They soon learned within one day that Mrs. Lorry was indeed not Mrs. Sackman! She was warm, permissive, creative, talkative, and extremely friendly and accessible to the children. The children went into a panic! Mrs. Lorry's tactics had been successful elsewhere but not here. These children had been disciplined and conditioned daily by the attitudes and methods of a cool martinet, and suddenly manna poured from the skies and the children couldn't handle it. They were frightened into a state of turmoil! All controls came off, and they made up for lost time, for the months they had spent under Mrs. Sackman's yoke!

A Plan for the Class

At this point, enter Mrs. Robbins, counselor, and the supervisor of the grade, Mr. Miller, who were both desperately called by Mrs. Lorry. The supervisor was dismayed at the turn things had taken and worked with Mrs. Robbins on a plan for action.

Group Discussion: It was decided to treat the class as a whole and meet with Mrs. Robbins several times a week to discuss the present state of affairs. At first, because of the bedlam, Mr. Miller remained to quiet down the youngsters so that they would listen. After a while they settled down and topics were then introduced for discussion, and ultimately even role-playing was conducted with the group (See Chapter Six). Among the topics discussed, pertinent to the present difficulties were:

   a. What does it mean to have a new teacher?
   b. All people are not the same, so teachers can be different too.
   c. Do we really want to behave in this fashion?

d. What do we want to learn in the class?

e. What plans does Mrs. Lorry have for us that we can be interested in?

f. What were we doing with Mrs. Sackman's class that we should like to continue?

g. Let's have a class project that we can all work on together (see unification project, Chapter Two).

Role-Playing: Children in the class role-played the part of the "New Teacher in the Classroom." It was an interesting variation from the year before when most of the class had role-played the "New Child in the Classroom" with a fourth-year teacher. The most disruptive children were deliberately chosen to play the role of the teacher. The children who had given Mrs. Lorry the most difficulty began to feel what it was like to be a new teacher when the rest of the class behaved badly. During the role-playing sessions, children in the group began to discipline one another so that the enactments could continue.

Class Modification: Richard, who had been Mrs. Sackman's strongest supporter, and Mrs. Lorry's greatest opponent, suddenly transferred his loyalties and Mrs. Lorry made him the leader of the class social studies project. He quickly rallied the forces of a small group he had selected. This coterie became the nucleus for other projects and kept the class rolling along. They had previously instigated the difficulty.

However, it took a while and the change of regime was gradual. Many of the children were suspicious of Mrs. Lorry's more democratic methods. They were not accustomed to participating in class management. Some never came along in the change of regime and resented Mrs. Lorry. They mentioned frequently that "Mrs. Sackman had to go have a baby!" But most readjusted to the new teacher. By May, children were working in small groups on individual projects and had forgotten about the chaos which reigned in February. The meetings with Mrs. Robbins terminated late in April, although occasionally she would drop in and see Mrs. Lorry and smile at the working children. In these visits Mrs. Robbins noted the decided change in the physical aspects of the room and the general tone.

A New Look: In contrast to Mrs. Sackman's class, where tables and chairs were arranged in straight rows, tables and chairs were placed in a semi-circle in Mrs. Lorry's, subject to further movement for group work. Where Mrs. Sackman's class was always quiet, Mrs. Lorry's had the noise of movement and low busy talking of children working on projects. Complete silence was not the order of the day and only occurred on formal occasions.

And it seemed to Mr. Miller, the supervisor, that the children looked much happier.

What really mattered was that the children were looking for consistency, and Mrs. Lorry, if anything, was consistently Mrs. Lorry. The children began to understand this difference.

Summary

The teacher and the counselor work together for the child but often have differences in directions and goals. These can be resolved by teachers and counselors working with each other through:

a. Understanding the different perceptions of each other's roles.
b. Individual Teacher-Counselor Conferences.
c. The Teacher-Counselor Discussion Group.
d. More Counselor Involvement in Class Functioning.

In understanding each other's roles, confusion, lack of knowledge and often resentment may accompany the teacher-counselor realtionship. The teacher often wants immediate change in terms of the child and the counselor deals in a longer range treatment concept.

The informal Teacher-Counselor conferences may provide for an ongoing workable classroom situation for the teacher with supportive help from the counselor. It will provide a plan for closer communication between the teacher and counselor.

The Teacher-Counselor Discussion Groups described here dealt with the frustrations of the minority child and with our own feelings as teachers and educators. The conclusions drawn were for expectations for the child's success and constructive handling of the frustrations of children and adults.

The counselor's involvement in the class situation is another way of opening up communication between teacher and counselor. The counselor, in this chapter, became an active member, for a time, of class 5-4 and its problems. Group guidance techniques were used by the counselor in giving the children insight into the problems and a class unification project, grouping activities and the use of class leaders advantageously by the teacher and counselor greatly improved the class's functioning and tone.

Chapter Four

A Teacher's Plea

I want you, my supervisor, to be an integral part of my classroom, not an outsider. Please help me, not suppress me; advise and support me, not merely direct me. I want to give you planning that is honest and prepare lessons that are meaningful to my children, and in exchange to be assisted to grow in my profession.

Working With the Administrator

The preceding words indicate the supervisor's key role in his or her relationship with the teacher. If he is guidance-minded, he will be supportive of his teachers and also of the parents and community.

Who is your administrator? How has his role changed over the years in the context of a changing school community? What is his relationship to yourself and to the parents of the children? How does he help you resolve the guidance problems within your classroom?

This chapter is going to attempt to answer these questions discussing the changing roles of your principal and your immediate supervisor, and putting you, for an instant, "in their shoes." It will show the importance of the teacher-supervisor relationships and will describe the guidance functions of the administrator as they relate to the teacher. We will trace the assistance given to a child in your class, Juan Martinez, initiating with a letter to the parent and terminating with the guidance conference, a step all make together.

Changing Roles in the School Community

The school community is in a state of flux. Roles have changed, not only of the involved parent but of teachers and supervisors as well. The trend is definitely that of increased interaction between teachers, supervisors and parents, and this greatly affects the child in the classroom

The Principal's Changing Role

The role of your principal has probably changed over the years. "Because of the increase of specialists in the school, the growing professional autonomy of teachers and the introduction of innovative programs, he has probably evolved from being a master of the curriculum to that of strategic coordinator."[1]

In order to coordinate the school into a functioning whole which operates smoothly, he may find himself with the additional function of something we will call "instant mediator" in terms of conflict between parents and teachers. This operates in the following manner:

A parent visits your school in an outraged state, informing your principal that a teacher has slapped a child. The more involved parent, a member of a more active community, cannot be easily shunted aside. Your principal instantly begins the mediation process between the child, parent and teacher, maintaining the precarious balance of not falling in the middle. This summons all the forces and innate charisma he can muster. For this proves to be one of the most precarious of juggling acts of the pedagogical world! To pacify an irate parent by listening to a possible list of invectives; to maintain a position of authority and yet indicate support of the parent; to admonish the teacher tactfully if this is needed, yet show support to teachers, to correct the parent, but not insult him or her; to point out the probability for error, yet accord the possibility that the parent may be right; and above all, to maintain a professional calm, is no small feat of maneuvering! Parents' involvement is growing along with the community's, and the principal's task is changing with it.

Teachers and Immediate Supervisors: Changing Attitudes

If you are to administer to the children's needs, then you want your own needs as teachers answered. Teachers now want more vital supervision. Mr. Miller, your supervisor, wistfully

---

[1] Adapted from Walter J. Kennedy, "The Changing Role of the Principal," *New York City Education* Issue Number 4 (Spring 1969), pp. 17-19.

remembers far simpler days when, twenty years before, as a new teacher, he had been given the following advice about supervisors:

- Try not to attract undue attention toward yourself.
- When you take a child to the supervisor, be aware that you may be casting a reflection upon yourself and your ability to handle a situation.
- Always hand in your plans on time. Then you won't attract too much attention if checked along with everyone else's.
- Don't display ignorance about curricula by asking too many questions.
- Definitely have a teacher relay system so that you know when the principal is coming and you can get the kids in their seats.

Does this sound a bit paranoiac? Perhaps much of this is operating in schools, but with a difference! There is a whole new regime of more vocal teachers rightfully seeking more direction relevant to the children's needs, assistance with the curriculum and children's problems, and yet who are paradoxically more autonomous in the classroom. Mr. Miller now has to deal with a new breed of teacher, with his needs and problems, a teacher who, unlike his former colleagues, will not make himself inconspicuous, and who will demand more meaningful answers to his questions.

Your Supervisor and You

The Teacher-Supervisor Relationship

Unfortunately, your supervisor has been stereotyped by current fiction. He has been cast as the "heavy." He has been portrayed as either a martinet or an intellectual misfit, disinterested in his teachers, concerned only with petty details, paperwork, and teacher lateness; he is tactless with teachers, a stifler of innovation and creativity, heartless toward children's needs and a general disciple of the school's bureaucracy. When we cast away that harsh and unfair piece of mythology, we find an individual who brings his or her own strengths and weaknesses to the position as others do. There are creative supervisors, dull ones, understanding ones, harsh ones, and those sensitive to the needs of children and teachers.

The relationship of the teacher with the supervisor has a profound influence in the teacher's relationship with the class. In one classroom, whenever the teacher had an altercation with the assistant principal, she let out her frustrations at the children. One astute child observed, "Mrs. Goldsmith is always so nice until she has a fight with Mr. Coleman. Then she yells at everybody!"

How do you perceive the supervisor, if you are the teacher? Undoubtedly many studies have been made, but if you listen to the voices of colleagues over a period of time, words pile up into needs, desires and perceptions, and perhaps unrealistic expectations:

I never forgot what Mr. King once told me. He said, "You really made little people out of those rough kids." I felt good for months after.

Supervisors should be able to tell you occasionally that you are doing a good job.

I rarely go to my supervisor, but when I do he usually takes the time to listen.

I'd like to feel the principal is supporting me all the way, even when the parents complain.

My supervisor is a marvelous woman. She plans with us all the way and really cares what goes on in each classroom.

What do I think? I'd like to be left alone! I told you before I never bother my supervisor or the counselor and handle my own problems. (Same teacher from Chapter Three.)

My supervisor is a great guy and concerned about teachers. He looks like Lincoln only his name is Levy.

It's about time someone asked me! I'll tell you what I want. I want a hidden camera taking pictures of the mamas' precious darlings to show parents what actually goes on in the classroom! My supervisor, Mr. Davis, said that I can have it granted in 1984 when Big Brother is watching.

Don't talk to me — I'm taking a transfer.

Don't kid yourself, the supervisor's job is really tough! I don't envy his job. He has to be everything to everybody.

What are you, a spy?

You know what really counts? It's what you do yourself in your classroom with nobody watching. It's what's real between you, your kids, and the Almighty!

You can see from the above remarks that teachers' attitudes toward supervisors range from admiration to indifference. As in all occupations, the personalities involved play a part in the teacher-supervisor relationship.

If the teacher has certain expectations of her supervisor, the administrator has similar expectations of the teacher:

The principal's view of his perfect teacher is one "who is a good classroom manager, conducts well-planned lessons to an orderly class, has a harmonious relationship with his colleagues and principal and has a warm, helping relationship with children leading to greater attention to individual pupil needs."[2] Creativity and initiative are rated behind these qualities.

The Making of a Teacher

Since you probably can't be all things to your principal or immediate supervisor, you will probably have to develop a certain personality in the classroom which is your own, capitalizing on your strengths and effectiveness in class management. Granted that certain manuals of learning quick techniques for class management and discipline may be helpful, they are not wholly realistic. Undoubtedly, good planning is essential for a smoothly running class, but if you are not the disciplinarian that your colleague is, and you try to be, your children will spot it fast enough. They will seek out the real you. If you are creative and not exacting in your approach, you will ultimately steer a more permissive creative course.

If you work with a supervisor who does not sanction new approaches, you will find that he will recognize your innovative strengths if you show persistence and talent in achieving your goals. Ultimately there must be a balance struck between what you are as a teacher and the guidance direction which a supervisor can provide. Good communication between yourself and your supervisor is undoubtedly the keynote.

The Supervisor in Guidance

How do you see your supervisor's role in guidance? How does

---

[2] Seymour Metzner, "The Teacher as Viewed by his Principal," *Changing Education* (A Journal of the American Federation of Teachers) Vol. 4, No. 3, 1969-70, p.25.

he work with your child in the classroom, with you as a teacher, with other school personnel, and with parents?

You, Mr. Cooper, sixth-grade teacher, have been having difficulties with Juan Martinez. You have been alarmed over the apparent lack of parent response to your notes and over a marked deterioration in Juan's work and behavior. You turn to Mr. Miller, your immediate supervisor, for help. He provides this help for you in the following ways:

Providing Relief

Juan is in trouble. He has hit a boy, refused to do homework, has been generally inattentive in class, and upon closer observation is moody and unhappy. When you called in Mr. Miller to break up a fight between Juan Martinez and Charlie Davis, you were thinking, "You've got to be tough, Mr. Miller, and make him afraid so that when I send him to you, he won't be so bad!" Mr. Miller understood this, but he also knew that punitive means for Juan would be short range. While speaking calmly with the boy, he made other plans.

Traffic Manager

Mr. Miller had to determine which road to take for Juan. This is the most difficult part of a supervisor's role. When he ascertained through conference with you that Mrs. Martinez was unable to be reached, then he took more drastic action and began to direct the proceedings.

Mr. Miller wrote a friendly note to Mrs. Martinez, requesting her to attend a conference in the guidance office to help plan for her son. He had the note translated into Spanish by Mrs. Colon, bilingual teacher, and both copies were mailed to the parent. This letter set the stage for future planning. If, as in this case, the tone of the note is a friendly one, it serves to unite the school and community by sharing in a common problem.

Now Mr. Miller contacts the counselor, Mrs. Robbins, to provide a guidance setting for the conference of Juan Martinez and to possibly provide therapy for the child and counseling for the family. He also involves the bilingual teacher in an attempt to bridge the gap between home and school. In making a home visit, Mrs. Colon reduces the mother's fear of the school situation so that she is prepared for the guidance conference.

A Preventor

In conferences which Mr. Miller has had with you, the child, parent and counselor, he has tried to intercept the child's behavior instead of waiting for the fateful explosion; he feels that Juan is on the verge of a more dramatic burst of behavior. He is concerned about the child's nervous mannerisms and his hyperactivity, and by seeking this conference, he attempts to ward off a more aggravated situation. The guidance conference, then, is a means of prevention.

A Conciliator

As a teacher of Juan, you had reached a point where you were terribly annoyed with the child who was disrupting the class, with a parent who did not respond, and with your supervisor whom you felt was not taking enough action. You let all this out in a burst of anger and were surprised when Mr. Miller waited for the explosion to pass and for you to calm down. He then began to take more direct action. You met with Mr. Miller again in a quiet discussion about the procedures to be taken and planned together for the guidance conference.

An Evaluator

Mr. Miller will evaluate the guidance directions he has taken. Will the guidance conference achieve the goals it has set out to reach? Juan's subsequent classroom behavior and academic performance will be gauged in terms of any slight or noticeable change. Changes in behavior will be long range and very slow and Mr. Miller is painfully aware of this.

The Guidance Conference: A Step Together

The guidance conference, which your supervisor may initiate and as the teacher you participate in, is one of the methods Mr. Miller uses in the guidance approach. In this conference the teacher, administrator, parent, counselor and child take a step together.

Teamwork between the teacher, guidance counselor and the supervisor is not a fully chartered course in the elementary school. Perhaps this is because the elementary school, still in its infancy in the field of guidance, is still groping with guidance techniques and with the role of the teacher, supervisor, and counselor working together.

The Guidance Conference for Juan Martinez

The administrative-guidance conference for Juan Martinez accomplished its immediate goals. It was a start and opened the door to future planning. The following transpired at the meeting:

Mrs. Martinez entered the conference quite fearfully. She had expected the worst. Mr. Miller, Mr. Cooper, Mrs. Colon and Mrs. Robbins all greeted her warmly, attempting to put her at her ease. They assured her (and Mrs. Colon stressed the point) that they were all there to help her child. After a silence, Mrs. Martinez whispered to Mrs. Colon, "I thought Juan's bad and everybody would yell!" She then partly relaxed and the meeting proceeded.

Mr. Miller introduced the subject of Juan (who was not yet present) in a friendly fashion, stressing the boy's assets. Mrs. Martinez seemed surprised and then pleased. Mr. Cooper continued the discussion and told her gently that he was concerned for the boy because, as his teacher, he wished the best for his progress.

During the discussion, Mrs. Martinez volunteered the information that Juan had come to this country not long ago and was unhappy here. She was mute, however, about further details of her situation, and was not pressed for information. (Juan was brought in at this point.)* Upon the suggestion of Mr. Miller, Mrs. Martinez agreed to play a more important role with Juan; she would check his homework each night as a start.

Through it all, Juan grinned nervously. He would not respond when gently asked to express his views of the meeting which had been called to help him.

The role of the counselor was explained by Mrs. Robbins, who arranged a private interview with Mrs. Martinez following the conference; Mrs. Martinez also agreed to meet privately with Juan's teacher, Mr. Cooper.

The meeting was concluded on a friendly note, but it might have been otherwise. It could have been a meeting in which

---

*It is a matter of opinion as to whether the child should be present during the entire meeting.

tensions were increased between home and school. In this respect the conference was a success.

The conference produced no miracles. It effected no metamorphosis in Mrs. Martinez; she remained fearful. It was no cure-all for Juan's ills; he continued his outbursts in the classroom and was still drowning in a sea of his own confusion.

But it was a beginning, a basis for constructive planning for Juan; the poeple involved could now take a step forward.

Suggestions for a Constructive Conference

There are many schools where good guidance conferences (and case conferences) take place in a warm and accepting manner. Mr. Miller learned after many disasters that there were important ingredients in à successful guidance conference.

1. A brief friendly letter of request to a parent to attend such a meeting.
2. Avoidance of a demanding, authoritarian tone in the communication to the parent. Keep the distinction between "urging" a parent to come to school because of the severity of the problem and "demanding" he come.
3. Parent is really listened to by all present and given full time to speak about what she or he deems important.
4. The good points of the child are always initially stressed by the teacher, counselor and supervisor. It is important not to tear down the child in the eyes of the parent or put the parent in a defensive position. (There are conferences in which the parent sometimes faces the unhappy task of castigating her child in front of the authority figures.)
5. A realistic picture is presented by the child's behavior, free from subjective interpretation by teacher, supervisor, or counselor.
6. The child does not witness confrontations between the parties involved.
7. The parent feels that the people at the conference are there to *help the child*.
8. The child feels that the people at the conference are there to help him or her.
9. The counselor, a participant in the conference, explains the guidance aspects of the conference, and indicates the need for further help to the parent, if necessary.

Summary

The teacher should work closely with the administrator, whether he is the principal or the immediate administrator of the grade. The administrator plays a large part in setting the tone of the school in his increasing involvement with teachers, parents, and children.

His relationship with his teachers has changed to one of more active participation in terms of their needs. The administrator plays an active role as part of a guidance team in helping the classroom teacher. He helps them in five ways: as a provider of emergency relief to teachers; as a traffic manager; as a preventor; as a conciliator; and as an evaluator.

As a preventor, he calls the guidance conference, and suggested here are ways to effect a successful one. The conference of Juan Martinez is used as an example.

Chapter Five

Dear Mrs. Martinez,

After our guidance conference in Mrs. Robbin's office I felt that I would like to meet with you again to speak of further planning for Juan's progress. I have free time on Wednesday, May 10, at 10:00 A.M. I hope this is convenient for you.

Yours sincerely,
Mr. Cooper — teacher of
class 6-2

Working With the Parent

There is a greater involvement today in working with parents, individually and in groups. The supervisor's role in providing the teachers with guidance-oriented techniques for handling parents, the parent-teacher conferences and the counselor-parent interviews are examples of this increased participation by all.

It is essential that you carefully plan meetings with parents under favorable conditions and avoid the pitfalls that these conferences are sometimes prone to.

Techniques for Teachers

When you greet parents in an individual interview or in group conferences you are, in large measure, involved in the counseling and guidance process. As a classroom teacher meeting the children's daily needs, you are the one most able to evaluate the child's strengths and limitations. The guidance approach with which you receive your parents affects your relationship with the child.

Your supervisor has probably given you suggestions for a parent-teacher conference. The purpose here is to stress those guidance aspects of the conference which may have been overlooked; the realm of attitudes plays a significant role.

Suggestions for Parent-Teacher Conferences

Before starting, approach the conference with a positive attitude. In cases of conferences which are required (such as those during open-school week) teachers may think of the situation "en masse;" it is a routine to be gotten over with. A room full of parents to be interviewed (if you are so fortunate to get such a response) can have the ingredients of an assembly line, One has to realize that each parent represents a child, and the interview is a marvelous device and potential for effecting change in the student. Take advantage of it!

Your interview has begun! A roomful of parents greet you, so—

Do:

1. Smile at the group, greeting them.
2. Sit parents at the back of the room.
3. Have a seating arrangement away from your desk to reduce the teacher authority image. You may sit at a small table, if you choose, in a private corner of the room.
4. First accentuate the positive about the child. (You cannot eliminate the negative but you can delay it.) Even your most severe behavior problem must have something positive about him There are few children without redeeming features (although you may disagree).
5. *Encourage the parent to talk; listen carefully not only to what is said but also to the manner, attitude and general feelings of the speaker.*[1]
6. Find out the reason for any parent concern and accept the explanation.
7. Plan together: One of the goals for you to work toward in counseling the parent is for the parent to take the initiative on her own. Suggestions toward helping the child should come mutually through discussion. You might introduce a plan of action by saying, "What do you think we can do?"
8. Listen calmly to possible complaints. (See the later section, "Complaints of Parents.") Give the parent a chance to vent her feelings.
9. Make a positive suggestion to the parent for a possible action she might take at the conclusion of the interview, and end the interview on an encouraging note about the child.

---

[1] *Guidance of Children in Elementary School* (Board of Education, City of New York. Curriculum Bulletin No. 13, 1955-56 Series), p.173.

Don't:

- rush the interview. It will probably take time for the parents to relax, tell what they are really worried about, and express their real feelings and fears.
- let comments about other children creep into the conversation.
- make comparisons with the student's brothers and sisters or with his classmates.
- "forget to write down the gist of what was discussed for future planning. Do this after the meeting."[2]
- push your own ideas on to an unready parent.
- register shock as to what the parent tells you.
- argue!
- and avoid psychiatric or psychological evaluations such as: "Your child is emotionally disturbed...," or probably retarded, brain-injured, paranoiac, anxiety prone, schizophrenic, hallucinating, aphasiac, or just plain crazy (even if the temptation is there!).

The guidance aspects of a parent-teacher conference are far-reaching. When you achieve a good relationship with the parent, there is a corresponding interaction between the parent and child. This undoubtedly affects the child's performance in school, and basically isn't that what you're really striving for?

About Guidance Problems

If parents of children with guidance problems are preparing to visit you, let the school counselor be aware of this. This feedback between you and the counselor about problem children, particularly in the area of parent visits, is important in any guidance program.

If problems arise during the conference which you can't handle, involving a particular child, you should likewise consult with the counselor.

Role-Playing Conferences

New teachers are frequently fearful of facing parents for the first time. The teacher, as the parent, does not know what to expect from the meeting. She frequently feels ill at ease, and unsure of what the attitude of the parent will be. As a new

---

[2]Adapted from *Working With Parents* (Washington, D.C.: National School Public Relations Association, 1201 Sixteenth Street, N.W., 1968), p.22.

teacher, I was suddenly faced with a hostile parent and groped for ways to handle the situation. This is more frequent than imagined. We somehow expect teachers to come to the classroom with a talent for handling all sorts of school situations. The teacher generally struggles at the outset before she acquires the techniques and the poise which become part of the pedagogical skills.

One method for preparing the new teacher for the parent-teacher conference is for the administrator (or counselor) to hold role-playing conferences, providing teachers with experience in interviewing parents.

The special problems, for example, of the parent with a complaint, the uncooperative parent, the hostile parent, and the working mother are themes that can be enacted.

Why Do Parents Come to School?

Parents are either summoned by the teacher or administrator (teacher-initiated) in answer to some problem about the child, or they come voluntarily (parent-initiated) for a variety of reasons, ranging from possible employment in the school, being a class mother, being a part of the parent association, accompanying a class on a trip, curiosity about the child's classwork, and frequently bearing and airing a complaint against the school and a particular teacher.

The Teacher-Initiated Interview

There are many reasons for a teacher-initiated interview with the parent. The interviews held during the school's parent-teacher conferences are initiated by the teacher, in which parents and teachers have a chance to get to know one another and plan for the child. Other conditions which warrant these interviews are children with excessive absences, who are doing badly in their classwork, who exhibit sudden strange changes in behavior, who have special talents which warrant additional training, and children who present severe behavior problems.

Disruptive behavior in the classroom, unfortunately, probably constitutes the basis for a good percentage of teacher-initiated interviews. It is unfortunate because the negative reinforcement of the parent toward the school situation comes again into play. This interview, however, similar to the guidance conference (Chapter Four), can be handled constructively for the child.

One Teacher-Initiated Interview: In the opening note of the chapter, Mrs. Martinez was sent a letter requesting her to visit the school. If you are Mr. Cooper, teacher of class 6-2, how do you handle your meeting with her?

First — you follow some of the suggestions for a "parent-teacher conference." You put Mrs. Martinez at her ease by sitting with her in a quiet corner away from your desk at a small table. In this way, you have eliminated the teacher-at-desk authority figure and you are physically equals. The room is quiet; it is your free period and the class has left for other instruction.

Then — when Mrs. Martinez is more composed, you discuss Juan and his problems. *You allow her to speak as much as possible.* She provides background about Juan: his wanting to return to Puerto Rico, his dislike of the slum area where he lives, his memory of childhood days.

Building on Strengths: Juan has strengths and you wish to build on them to establish a basis for rapport and planning.

He is bright and alert, he draws well, has leadership qualities and is learning the language quickly. You show Mrs. Martinez his art work on exhibition in the hallway; you indicate that his leadership qualities can be a force for good in the classroom. You stress that to be bilingual is desirable and in retaining the Spanish, he will feel a transition between the two cultures.

Planning: You discuss Juan's quick temper and aggressive fighting with other boys. You have attempted, with some success, to intercept Juan's outbursts by a prearranged signal to him. Since he shows manual dexterity, you have engaged him in projects in which he uses his hands. Juan has a need for learning self-control and re-channeling of his energies.

Juan's feeling of displacement is compounded by his unhappiness. Mrs. Colon, the bilingual teacher, and Mrs. Robbins, the counselor, have entered Juan into an activity group at a Spanish Cultural Center near his home. His reluctance to attend quickly changes into eagerness.

You discuss the need that Juan has for additional help. Mrs. Martinez and Juan have set further appointments with the counselor. You know that there is much that Mrs. Martinez has not revealed and she appears very troubled. She admits to an urgent need for family counseling, which she fears.

Opening the Door: Whatever resistance Mrs. Martinez had about entering the school has been dissipated through subsequent meetings. You have begun to plan constructively with her; Mr. Martinez has also paid you a visit. You know that Juan still requires a great deal of help, but appropriate steps have been taken with the parents' cooperation. As the teacher of Juan, concerned with his problems on a daily basis, you offer him guidance; you're opening the door to future planning.

The Parent-Initiated Interview

In the foregoing section we discussed Teacher-Initiated Interviews, but many times parents make their way into school with a complaint either against the teacher or teaching methods. What are these complaints? How does the teacher deal with them?

Complaints of Parents: "I never see a reader taken home. What are these children doing?"

"You give much too little homework!"

"You give homework they had last year!"

"You're always blaming my child. What about the other children?"

"Why aren't teachers allowed to hit? I give my permission."

"My child said that you hit him!"

"You're not strict enough with the children. They walk all over you!"

"I never learned math that way. It's a crazy system."

"I'm going to speak to the assistant principal about having her class changed. I don't want her in your class. I had no trouble with her last year in Mrs. Stillman's class. She understood her."

"I had no trouble with him in the other school. Since he has been in this school, he does nothing but fight!"

"Let me tell you about this here school. The principal does nothin', the supervisor does nothin', the counselor does nothin', and the teachers don't do nothin' — that's why the kids do nothin', and it won't be investigated because the mayor of this here city does nothin'."

Are All Complaints Valid? Not all are, yet complaints cannot be sloughed off. They must be dealt with, and this is a sensitive task for the classroom teacher. What makes the complaints exceedingly difficult to handle is that at times they are a mask for other problems which the parent has. She may have projected family problems upon the school situation.

Many complaints may be just symptoms of poor school-home communication. When a closer relationship can be established between the parent and teacher, the complaint disappears.

The parent may be looking for recognition from the school for herself and her child for some underlying reason. Parents as well as teachers and children still have the need for self-importance. These are the very parents who should be channeled into the school organization, such as the parent association, to provide an outlet for worthwhile activities.

There are, however, certain kinds of actions which the teacher can take to successfully handle parents' complaints.

How Do You Handle Complaints?

- *Stay Calm!* If your heart pounds at the sight of a scowling, agitated parent, try to maintain control!

- *Listen to the Complaint.* (If you can muster up sympathy, so much the better.) If possible, try to have the parent meet with you somewhere away from the ears of the class before listening to the problem. In this way, the heat of anger will have abated somewhat and you don't have an audience.
  NOTE: There is nothing quite as agitating to a class than to see a parent and teacher in a heated exchange.

- If there is a question about the curriculum, invite the parent to sit in on a lesson.

- A good strategic device is to involve a hostile parent in being a class mother or volunteering to assist in class projects, providing of course that she is not working. One very vocal parent who was employed became involved in a school bazaar; this event was held on a Saturday afternoon in the schoolyard.

- Try not to throw the blame entirely onto the parent for the shortcomings of the child. Use the pronoun "we," for example, to designate the school's share of the responsibility.

- Involve other personnel in serious complaints you cannot handle yourself. The supervisor or counselor can be brought in for clarification of an issue such as an aspect of the curriculum.
- Meeting the parent half-way will allow her to modify the complaint. She may be correct in her assumption that you are picking on Willie. You may indicate this, but isn't it possible that he is constantly causing you to do so? You will find that she will probably admit to this.
- "A soft answer turneth away wrath." As a teacher and counselor, I have found few exceptions — if you meet anger with a gentle tone (which takes practice) the anger slowly dissipates; meeting anger with your own anger is sure to cause a conflagration.
- The thing for you to remember as a teacher is that it is far more difficult for the parent to enter the school than for you, for it is your familiar domain! By the time the parent arrives she may have much feeling stored up and in releasing it a potential conflagration may ensue. Clearing the air, however, can be very beneficial, if handled constructively.
- Repeated conferences with parents are the best means for nullifying complaints.

Can We Meet the Needs of Parents?

As the child and teacher have special needs, so does the parent. The teacher, supervisor, and counselor can help direct a more positive attitude of the parent toward the school.

Can we meet the need for positive reinforcement of the parent's attitude by teachers and supervisors?

The teacher can assist in this by informing the parent when the child achieves or is engaged in an interesting class or school project. Parents of recalcitrant youngsters should be notified when the child has shown some success. Failure becomes easier to accept when there is a backlog of success to cushion it.

Can we meet the need of the parent for understanding of the environment in which he or she functions?

The teacher can gain knowledge of the home conditions of

the parent at a time mutually agreed on by the teacher and parent. Crowded home conditions, the single parent home, and the lack of suitable facilities for studying, are all problems affecting the child.

Can we meet the parents' need for understanding of school policies?

In one community "the parents' misunderstanding and negative opinions of the school program was considerably decreased when an administrator and some of his teachers met with a group of parents an evening a week for ten weeks to discuss the goals of education."[3]

Can we deal with new social trends, such as that of the working mother?

The working mother, a growing phenomonon, must be dealt with at times convenient for her. Many women cannot take time from work to meet with a teacher during the day, and many widowed and divorced single parents have no sitter at night to watch younger children. In one school, teachers (and counselor) come to class a half-hour earlier to speak with the working parent; in another, the parent visits in the home of the teacher or in the home of another parent (taking offspring with them). Of course, the traditional home visit by the teacher to the parent would be of growing importance in this situation.

Can we meet the need for recognition and participation of the parent in the school?

Involvement in parent workshops, parent association meetings, and parent steering committees in the school have helped toward meeting this need. In one school a parent-guidance group was developed, composed of volunteer parents working with recalcitrant guidance problems designated by the teacher, counselor, and supervisor. These were children whose parents were either ineffectual in dealing with them, or showed little interest in their behavior. Under the direction of the counselor, they visited the homes of these youngsters, influencing many of these parents to come up to school to discuss the children. The parents of this guidance group also related individually with the youngsters in a kind of pseudo-parent relationship. The parent-guidance group

---

[3] Ruth Strang and Glyn Morris, *Guidance in the Classroom* (New York: The Macmillan Company, 1964), pp.89-90.

worked out surprisingly well and effected a closer relationship with the community.

How the Counselor Works With the Parent

As the teacher, you may wonder about what goes on inside the guidance office when one of your parents visits the counselor. You may ask the counselor the following:

What happened between you and the parent?
Did she tell you anything that may help me?
What are you trying to do?
How will the meeting help me to handle the child?

The following is a meeting which took place between Mrs. Martinez, the parent, and Mrs. Robbins, the counselor. Perhaps this brief glimpse into the guidance office will provide the teacher with an answer to some of these questions.

The Counselor-Parent Interview

Mrs. Martinez sat in Mrs. Robbins' office very distressed and confused. Mrs. Robbins sat in a chair away from her desk, facing the small woman who was tearfully recounting problems in her marriage and ambiguous feelings twoard her son. She paused to sip a cup of tea which Mrs. Robbins had made for her. It was her first interview with the counselor.

Rapport: An important word in the counseling interview is rapport, and this is what Mrs. Robbins seeks to achieve with Mrs. Martinez. This is the same rapport that you, the teacher, try to achieve with the parent during the parent-teacher conference. Mrs. Robbins seeks to enlist Mrs. Martinez's confidence in order to effectively bring her to a point where she will be willing to seek outside help from an agency, help her family desperately needs.

In subsequent discussions with Mrs. Robbins, Mrs. Martinez continually stressed her conflicts in feeling toward her son. He had come from Puerto Rico two years before, and caused growing differences between herself and her new husband. She had left him as a young child with her mother in Puerto Rico, and had come to the United States to reestablish herself after an unhappy marriage. Mrs. Martinez is torn between keeping Juan and sending him back; Juan loves his mother and vacillates between staying with her and returning to Puerto Rico.

Agency Referral: Mrs. Robbins referred Mrs. Martinez and her family to a community agency, where she was given a Spanish therapist. Her husband, resistant at first to family counseling, finally agreed to go when he realized the seriousness of the problem.

Juan was given individual psychological evaluation and therapy at the same agency.

Did These Interviews Help? After several conferences with Mrs. Martinez, Mrs. Robbins had a better understanding of the child's problems so that she was able to suggest to you, the teacher, methods of handling Juan.

The family had been referred to a treatment center to be able to deal with the source of the difficulty and provide for a better setting for Juan to function.

Individual help for Juan and intensive therapy had been effected. Hopefully this would improve his school functioning.

Summary

Today, there is a greater involvement by teachers, supervisors and guidance counselors in working with parents than in the past.

The supervisor provides techniques for his teachers for effective parent-teacher conferences. Development of positive attitudes in the teacher-parent meeting directly affect the performance of the child in the classroom.

Effective ways to handle complaints of parents by teachers help to mollify an aggravated and potentially destructive situation.

The parents' needs must be met in terms of the school and the child. New ways to reinforce positive attitudes of the parents toward the school, parents' understanding and participation in school matters, and the school's accomodation to new social trends, such as the working mother, had to be dealt with.

The counselor, in working with the parent, helps the teacher. Referrals for individual therapy and family counseling hopefully will improve the child's functioning in the classroom.

Chapter Six

Dear Diary

Today is monday and I played a mommy. Amy played my little girl. She didn't do her homework so I spanked her. Amy cryed and hit me. That's not fair. Little girls shudent hit there mommys. Next time I want to be a teacher so I can yell at the bad children.

Using Creative Dramatics and Role-Playing in the Guidance of Children

All children play. You as the teacher have observed this many times. The perceptions of children of life around them, given impetus by their imagination and creativity, gradually develop simple play activities into dramatic play and creative dramatics. Ultimately the more formal, structured dramatic art takes form, with set, plot and dialogue. It is through the spontaneity of the dramatic play and creative dramatics that the children learn to assess themselves and their conclusions. The playing of varied roles in dramatic play also becomes the springboard for role-playing activities of a problem-solving nature.

All children benefit from these dramatic forms, the advantaged as well as the disadvantaged, the troubled as well as the placid child. You as the teacher can help these children by utilizing these guidance tools. The eventual gaining of insights by the youngsters into their own behavior and modification of their actions will be a reward for this maturing process.

Try Pantomime at First

Little Clarence sits at the third table in your kindergarten class. You've scarcely ever heard him utter a word. His eyes look troubled as he occasionally glances at you for approval. If you have a guidance counselor in your school, Clarence had probably been seen and referred by the guidance service to a speech pathology unit in a local hospital. His problem may be physical or psychogenic in nature. This has not yet been determined. He has been getting both a physical and psychological work-up.

Clarence, however, wants with all his heart to be an integral part of the class. He participates in class dramatic play, but you are surprised to see him pantomime instead of speak. He feels comfortable in this medium, and this is fine and should be encouraged. Mime is a good base for all dramatic activities. It can be used successfully by the first-grade as well as the sixth-grade students, the non-English speaking child, the withdrawn child and the child who pathologically does not speak, such as Clarence. At this point, through pantomime, Clarence feels secure in his dramatic activity and he should not be pressured into verbalizing. He will do this when he is ready for it. As his teacher you have probably set the stage for pantomime without realizing it. You may have had your class do group pantomime such as skipping, hopping and rhythms, and when Clarence galloped like a horse he felt a tremendous physical release.

Preparing for Pantomime

Here are some additional suggestions which can prepare the way for pantomime by stimulating the children:

Creative Dance: Play a melodious selection such as "The Waltz of the Flowers" from the "Nutcracker Suite" by Tschaikovsky and have the children paint their impressions of the music by body movement. The creative dance is an expressive type of pantomime.

Play a contrasting selection such as any military march or a spirited piece such as "The Russian Sailors' Dance" from the ballet "The Red Poppy" by Gliere. Have the children show the increase in tempo of the piece by body movement until the crescendo at the finish.

Character Pantomime: Play the favorite themes from "Peter and the Wolf" by Prokofiev. The entire selection should be played several times to acquaint the class with the characters, and themes for the various characters and story. Children are then chosen to pantomime each character from the selection — Peter, the grandfather, the cat, the bird, the wolf, the duck and the woodsman. Then, when the theme is played, the appropriate character will pantomime his or her interpretation of the role. The children will enjoy identifying their roles with the themes played, rather like a game. "Peter and the Wolf" can be further expanded into an improvisation at a future time. It lends itself, excellently, to music, creative dramatics and art activities.

Machine Parts: Be part of a machine. Synchronize different parts of the machine as they are pantomimed by the children. This can develop into a highly unusual and entertaining experience involving motor control and precise teamwork as the children accelerate and slow down together. This is recommended for the middle grades, where children have more motor control.

Fantasy Play: What are you? Who are you? Indicate by gestures what your job is.

Pick someone you see on the street each day and pretend you are that person. The children will bring to the pantomime their own cultural and environmental milieu.

Choose an animal and pretend you are that animal. This is particularly suitable for kindergarten and first-grade children.

Dramatic Play—A First Step in Dramatics

You as the teacher in the kindergarten and early grades probably have dramatic play situations each day in your classroom. Encourage this dramatic play to be free and unhampered. You will see that if encouraged, it will provide a release for Clarence's most urgent needs and encourage him to verbalize.

Dramatic play might also provide an outlet for your aggressive John, the class bully, to react to his inner conflicts in a socially acceptable way. He may attempt to beat a rubber baby doll and thereby vent his anger at having been beaten himself the night before. He has come to school from a slum area, a distance away. His dramatic play is spontaneous, as are his feelings. John needs no script to characterize his feelings. His play is the play of all children, a will-o-the-wisp type of thing, taking its cue from the whims and emotions of the children at the moment. John has played a scene over and over again, each time with a slightly altered outcome; each time there is a new twist. He is looking for some new solution for his difficulties, a magic key to future action. This dramatic play is helping John to develop awareness and sensitivity.

Your shy Wanda has re-enacted a mother and daughter role in a play situation involving misbehavior and punishment. Wanda has played the mother and daughter role alternately with perky little Karen, who sits at her table. With each new enactment in free play, Wanda has altered her performance as she perceives different solutions to her roles. But in this unstructured situation, there must be some order and warmth to allow the children an opportunity to express themselves fully.

Little Maria Gonzales in your class arrived from Puerto Rico a few months ago. She has had difficulty with English as a second language and speaks to her dolls in both Spanish and English. Because her mother speaks Spanish in the home, she does likewise when she assumes a mother role. Maria reverts back to English when she plays the role of the daughter. This dramatic play is helping her to verbalize more articulately in both tongues and in communicating with another child through a play situation. Her speaking in Spanish should not be thwarted at the onset, for this is the way she makes a transition to a new cultural and language situation. She will retain the Spanish as another language and gradually absorb the new language. Ideally, of course, she should be getting special tutoring in English on some special basis.

Creative Dramatics — The Plot Thickens and Characters Speak!

In the first and second grades a transition is slowly being made in the unstructured dramatic play situations. They are becoming a base for creative dramatics. By the middle grades this new dramatic form has emerged if a certain accepting climate has been set for the children. The story line of the dramatic play has become more structured and dialogue is improvised to fit this developing plot.

Using Improvisation

What do we mean when we speak of an improvisation? We are referring to a situation which is developed and enacted with spontaneous dialogue. If the dialogue is not spontaneous when enacted, it is not an improvisation and not creative dramatics. As we will discuss later, this improvisation may be based on a pre-written story, but in the final enactment the children must interpret their own dialogue.

With the improvisation of dialogue, characterization is shaping up and children are selected in advance to portray roles. This all sounds fairly simple, but when attempting your first improvisation you might find that it is unexpectedly clumsy. You may have a momentary setback. Children who seemed eager to perform are suddenly hesitant and self-conscious, whether in the classroom or guidance office. You can expect your children with speech defects and language stumbling blocks to be reticent about verbalizing. You had expected the self-confident child to take the initiative in the dramatization, but he also seems reluctant at first. If you are not critical of the performance or lack of performance, and allow the children to develop dialogue with a minimum of direction, the beginning self-consciousness will fade.

When you are considering creative dramatics as a medium of expression, it is important, I have found, to honestly assess the kind of teacher you are and your rapport with your class. This may be difficult to do, but the degree of group interaction and participation is essential in creative dramatics. In some classes, creative dramatics will just not flourish. You will be able to enact a routine play with various pre-written parts assigned in a right atmosphere, but creative development may not be your cup of tea. Children need a warm, accepting, non-critical atmosphere. Your own enthusiasm for the project will also play a part. The children get the message very quickly and are quite perceptive.

If you have an extremely permissive classroom, care should be taken in having small groups used in creative dramatics while planning activities for the remainder of the class.

Creative Dramatic Situations

What kinds of children do you teach? Are they ghetto, suburban, or rural? The nature of these children will influence you as to the nature of the situations used for improvisations. However, certain situations could be applicable to children from all environments:

1. "You have found a kitten that you want very much to keep but

your mother has said that you cannot have a pet. Try to persuade her that the kitten needs a home.

2. You are moving to a new neighborhood today. Your best friend comes around to your home to say goodbye to you. Although you are looking forward to your new home, you are sad to leave the old neighborhood. What do you say?

3. Your mother has given your old rag doll to your younger cousin who is visiting you. Neither of them knows how much the doll means to you. You pretend it is all right.

4. You are a group of people in a subway station. It is six o'clock in the evening. In the center is a newsstand, at which newspapers, magazines, and candy are sold. It is run by a woman who has been there for many years. She knows the passengers who ride regularly, and is interested in them and all the details of their daily lives. Decide on the person you are going to be — a policeman, an actress, a shopper, etc. Then let us know all about you through your conversation with the proprietor of the newsstand, while you are waiting for your train."[1]

5. How would a group of people react if they were caught in an elevator, a bus, etc.?

6. Pick a color. How would you react if you were that color? Express through words the feelings about that color. The teacher should avoid stereotyped responses.

Initiating a Creative Dramatics Group

You are a teacher in the early grades and you are attempting creative dramatics for the first time. You have to cope with distractions, noise, unruly children and even monitors interrupting with messages.

You may wonder then, of what value is all this for the child? You realize that it is a natural medium from both a guidance and therapeutic point of view. You think of your children, disruptive Eric and withdrawn Shari, and how they will react to such a group. Eric's own background would provide a veritable storehouse of material. His difficulties, which in part may be of a social nature, will manifest themselves in this creative activity.

You initiate a group and Eric and Shari become a part of it. Shari would only be with the group physically at first. She then

---

[1] Nellie McCaslin, *Creative Dramatics in the Classroom* (New York: David McKay Company, Inc., 1968), pp. 56-57.

pantomimed a bit, once as a mean mother screwing up her little face, rolling her saucer-shaped eyes. Within a few months, however, she projected herself into the role of a very pretty daughter.

Eric, who always browbeat Shari in your class situation, was genuinely confused. He didn't accept Shari's growing stature as a personality and was puzzled by it. Shari had become the popular heroine in the dramatic group, a part she always yearned to play in real life. Eric, surprisingly enough, after a few aggressive motions with his fist, settled down and became subdued. He was no longer the Eric of the classroom, an aggressive bully. The children had literally reversed roles in the dramatic situation. It was a metamorphosis brought about by creative expression!

Improvisations Based on Original Stories

Although it is much safer to base the improvisation on a well-known story, and certainly far simpler, the reward of original endeavor, in terms of stimulating the child's imagination, is worth the effort. Unfortunately, in many of our elementary school classrooms, the stress on the unusual and original is frowned upon and not developed. Dr. E. Paul Torrance, in *Rewarding Creative Behavior* states, "In most classrooms the child who expresses a new or unusual idea not in the books takes a calculated risk. In such a setting, it takes a great deal of courage for a child to press for presentation of his unusual ideas."[2]

Developing a Scene

In the early grades, it will be too difficult to plan a complete play. At best, these children will develop a single scene rather than a complete plot. You may start by giving the class practice in original plot development by the introduction of the unfinished story situation and character development. The children may create these stories and characters or they may be selected from stories they know. These characters will be put into a changed setting and an improvisation developed.

In original improvisations in the early grades, simplicity is the

---

[2] E. Paul Torrance, *Rewarding Creative Behavior* (Englewood Cliffs, N.J.: Prentice-Hall, Inc., 1965), p.316.

keynote. It is only through class discussion, and eliciting of responses recorded on experience charts for clarification, that an improvisation can take form. Something which is different and unique may have happened to one of the youngsters. When sufficient discussion has taken place in an orderly fashion, it is your place as the leader to guide the children into choosing the ideas which seem most promising. Children who seemed most enthusiastic in the development of this material will be chosen to play the scene. Little or no scenery is required in an improvisation. If necessary, a simple prop may be used for the younger child.

Improvising a Story

In the middle grades, a story such as Cinderella may be held up as an example in terms of a theme, characters and some resolution of plot. Cinderella may be simply diagrammed showing the three scenes that comprise it: the scene at home, the scene at the ball, and the scene at the end when Cinderella is finally united with the prince.

In these middle grades, the unfinished story based on original ideas or the selection of characters from some book or play being read, will again be used as with the younger child. A single scene will be improvised using characters selected in a changed setting, as was noted above. The children, in selecting the characters with whom they identify, will try to retain some consistency in characterization although the circumstances have changed. This again gives the children an insight into the influence characterization has upon plot development. Discussion should follow the various enactments to determine whether the characters acted appropriately. With new enactments the characterization will become more detailed and there will be changes in interpretation.

A creative fifth grade teacher, Mrs. Teller, developed a delightful character in group collaboration with her class. (You will meet Mrs. Teller again in Chapter Thirteen, "Guidance Through Creativity," where she sets out to write a story with her class.) In the dramatization of the unfinished story situation, ideas were elicited from the class as to the types of characters they would like to portray, and the following characters and situation evolved:

FIGURE 6-1

A rather odd-looking bookseller, (see Figure 6-1) stood in his musty old shop. He held a huge pocket watch which he pulled out of his vest pocket at intervals from time to time, shaking his head and muttering to himself. He had glasses at the tip of his nose which he totally disregarded because he always looked over the top of them. Four children were in the shop looking for various books. Then suddenly the door opened slowly and a highly suspicious-looking, shabbily dressed individual walked in very cautiously.

The bookseller was interpreted differently in the subsequent enactments by the class. He was old and then young, conservative and then very modish. He looked at his watch because he was late to dinner and he had a nagging wife; he looked at his watch because this was simply a nervous habit. One whimsical boy recreated a scene worthy of Alice in Wonderland. He muttered, "Well-well-well! How very real!" everytime he pulled out his watch from an imaginary vest pocket with a grand sweeping gesture. When questioned by one of the children what it was that was real, he answered, "Everything is real except this watch and perhaps you. I'm not sure!" The children found it difficult to continue because of the laughter from the rest of the class.

The suspicious-looking individual who came into the store developed into a very amiable and respectable old man, a bit lonely, looking for a book to buy; in another enactment he became a pirate on the high seas. He dragged a wooden leg a la Captain Hook in Peter Pan. The dramatizations proved memorable.

Exploring Plot

In a gifted class more detailed mechanics of playwriting such as plot, climax and denouement can be explained. The class on a group, or preferably individual basis, may attempt to create a one-act play with no more than three scenes. The ideas will be submitted in written form and a noteworthy language arts lesson may develop. Discussion will then follow, with different ideas considered for improvisation. These ideas will be recorded for possible future improvisations. An accepting teacher will welcome all ideas, however unattractive they may appear. Some skits are composites of different ideas submitted; however, this is difficult to integrate. The story with resolution of plot will usually be very difficult to manage except with very bright children.

However, we still have pioneer teachers! There are those educators who are very venturesome or extremely skillful in guiding the very slow child in creative enterprises. They will create a one-act play with a difficult class and successfully make it into an exciting improvisation.

Improvisations Based on an Established Story

You may have found that the creating of original material for improvisation is too difficult for your class. Then the established story is better suited for you. You have chosen "The Sleeping Beauty" for improvisation because it is a familiar tale.

How good are you as a storyteller? Your retelling of the story to the class and your manner of reading it will be important in motivating them for their interpretation. In the retelling of the story some dialogue should be read so that the children get the flavor of the characters. After the children are reacquainted with the tale, they may establish by discussion the main scenes of the story. It is best to play the story in small units. "Each scene of a play may involve several small incidents. The festive first scene in The Sleeping Beauty includes the preparation for the feast, the arrival of the guests, their gifts for the princess, the appearance of the wicked fairy and her curse,   and the conclusion with the good fairy's softening of the princess' fate. Each little part is played several times with different casts before putting it together, so that by the time the complete scene is played, some of the details have been worked out and the characters have been established."[3]

In the re-enactments, then, different children will get an opportunity to engage in different roles. It is there where children may enact parts which may be secretly coveted in real life. The plain girl should be the one given the opportunity to play the beautiful heroine. Unfortunately, all of us remember incidents from our childhood where the most popular children were always the ones chosen to play the leading parts. How much talent must have been buried in our quiet, creative children! Since improvisation does not need an audience and does not have as its aim dramatic perfection, full reign should be given to children to express themselves.

Children Color Improvisations

In building an improvisation on a story theme, some adherence should be given to the basic plot of the original story. However, individual children will bring their own experience and background to the interpretation. If a story like Hansel and Gretel or Cinderella is used, the rural child's improvisations will be colored by his own bucolic experiences. Little Cinderella might feed the chickens and milk the cows if played by country children, but for the urban child her housework might be that of sweeping the apartment or tenement. Cinderella might be relegated to the role of a servant in the house as seen by an affluent child. Slum conditions might color the dialogue of a ghetto child, and his own perception of individuals and environment will influence plot and character development.

---

[3] Winifred Ward, *Playmaking with Children* (New York: Appleton-Century-Crofts, Meredith Corporation, 1957), p.135.

In a small creative dramatics group in your ghetto class, for example, John became a very pugnacious page of the prince. He held the glass slipper quite arrogantly and scolded the wicked stepsister with, "Man, I don't like the way I see you make Cinderella do all them jobs, and if you open your mouth I'm goin' to bust it for you!" With that he yanked the glass slipper from the stepsister's foot. Little, vivacious Karen made a swinging motion to hit him, which you intercepted in time. The children had projected themselves into the characters.

About Puppetry

It is difficult to discuss the field of creative dramatics without a brief look at puppetry. When a child is withdrawn, physically handicapped or very disturbed, puppetry provides a cloak to hide self-consciousness. As the teacher, you gain insight into children's problems through this spontaneous dramatization. It will be advisable to note not only the dramatic aspects of puppetry, but its interrelationship with the arts and crafts program. (For further information about puppetry, see Chapter Seven, "Guiding Children Through Art Experiences.")

Improvisation for the Disadvantaged

Improvisation is a tremendous medium for the exchange of ideas, not only for the average and gifted child but for the disadvantaged child as well. The child from the ghetto has a tremendous potential for responding to situations with language that is quite original. He is imaginative in an unorthodox way, with a rich use of expressive motions and adjectives. This is unfortunately an area which is frequently untapped by the teacher. The child brings to his creative playing a rich source of material — his background.

A Class Creation

Disadvantaged children in a fourth-grade class combined efforts in a creative enterprise. They improvised dialogue to an original unfinished story they called, "Trouble In Heaven." The story was as follows: Each child was to choose a character whom he or she admired. That character was to tell of accomplishments in order to gain access into heaven. These could be real or imaginary persons. Little skits were then improvised and developed from the characters selected. Since this was a class in a ghetto area, the children chose members of minority groups to identify with. In the case of the ghetto child, it raised his aspirational level to model himself after an admired adult. Children from other backgrounds are not so dissimilar. They too need a person to identify with, as identification is a natural process of growing up.

In the improvisation, the dialogue and situations in this instance were awkward at first, and not in keeping with the characters selected. You may encounter a similar difficulty in respect to other characterizations. You must refrain from interfering and give the children a great scope in the development of characters and situations. Some interesting revelations of children's perceptions of people and of themselves will emerge if not thwarted.

It must be noted that although this improvisation was based upon original ideas stemming from the children, you may base your improvisation on established themes, such as familiar fairy tales. This may be easier to develop in many ghetto classrooms.

Role-Playing

In our discussion of dramatic play, one of its values is the exploration of conclusions or decisions which the child arrived at in repeated re-enactments. This is a similar base for role-playing. Role-playing is a type of improvisation, a way of letting children engage in reality situations, usually social, involving the handling of a particular problem. It serves to explore children's feelings and to elicit different solutions and their consequences. Teachers are not therapists and the purpose of role-playing is not toward this end; it is rather the exploration of conflict situations with which the child is confronted and the manner in which they can be met. There are other purposes of role-playing, but this is the one we are primarily concerned with here. Teachers and guidance counselors will find it an excellent tool for social growth, each applying its results differently.

Class 4-2 and Role-Playing

You are the teacher of class 4-2, a very volatile group of fourth-grade youngsters. Role-playing looms up as a fascinating yet fearful medium because you have not tried it. You have many problems in your class involving interpersonal relationships. When you had given a sociogram (see Chapter Nine, "The Sociogram"), you had found that your class lacked cohesiveness. John and Eric are constantly fighting with one another; both are bullies. Your class is an integrated one, a mixture of racial groups which are having difficulty mixing from time to time. The entire class reflects these tensions. Some black children, like John, bussed in from slum areas, have a difficult time relating to the white middle-class youngsters, like Eric, and are asserting themselves more than necessary. A few Spanish children, newly arrived from Puerto Rico, are getting coached in English, yet are still having a difficult time with the new language. They also still feel the newness of a strange environment and have difficulty in adjusting. Some of the children resent these "interlopers" and feel that they do not belong to the class. Feelings occasionally run very high. The work becomes slower in pace, at times, accommodating all the children. Sue is a bright quiet girl who has suddenly stopped doing her homework. Her mother, an educated woman, blames the situation on the mixture of the class. She intends to come to school to have Sue's class changed to one with "more motivation." A few slower white children have their own private world in the back of the room, and note passing and verbal exchanges are their steady diet. In the sociogram, they presented a chain and you are not sure yet how to manage their seating. You suddenly realize that, taking everything into consideration, you are only teaching to a small nucleus of the class. Only this group is actually listening to you.

There is little question as to why you would be afraid in a group such as this to attempt a new medium! Yet, the guidance counselor and a very guidance-minded supervisor have recommended role-playing to you.

Setting the Proper Tone

How do you go about role-playing? At the beginning you are not going to determine which children have dramatic ability. Your aim is social growth and not dramatic excellence. It is necessary to be nonjudgmental. A neighboring teacher tried role-playing, but she was so critical of the children's performances that they consequently became acutely self-conscious.

You also know that John and Eric will probably try to take over the situation with their aggressiveness, and you will have to deal with this constructively. Yet, you must be non-directive in your approach.

Key Steps for Role-Playing

Here are the key steps in going about initiating a role-playing experience:

Introducing the Problem

You choose a problem applicable to your class situation. Two new children enter your class from another neighborhood. One is black, one is Spanish. They meet in the schoolyard, after school, with some of the other children in the class. These children are playing stickball and jumping rope. How do all the children see this situation? How do you think they feel? What do you think is going to happen? (These questions will be asked of the children of the class.)

The Environment

The environment consists of selecting the players, setting the stage, and preparing the audience.

The players in this particular class should be selected with an eye to having children take contrasting roles. White children should assume the roles of the new children and a child such as John, for example, should represent the status quo. A stage will be simply set in such a way that the rest of the class has a clear view of the action, and can participate later.

Preparing the audience in this classroom might be a most important point because these children are not attentive. They must be made to feel that they are an important part of the enactment since their cooperation afterwards is essential. The approach should be one of elevating their function rather than reprimanding them for inattention.

The Enactment

You are now the leader of this role-playing situation. The players are standing in the school yard. John is holding a pointer for a bat, and an eraser as a ball. You are uneasy because you picture that eraser flying out of the window! Eric has become the new boy, and one false move between him and John may prove disastrous! The children are also beginning to feel the first pangs of self-consciousness. John and Eric suddenly smile sheepishly, completely out of character. The other characters shift their feet nervously! However, you make a start by questioning each player in turn what he or she is thinking about. At first, they don't respond and you feel like giving the whole affair up. Then an unexpected thing happens — Quiet Sue, in the role of the little Spanish girl, admonished Linda for not letting her play rope with the other little girls. Eric follows suit and turns to John and accuses him of not letting him play in the game. Sue, then, with a burst of authority, turns on the other players. Sue, of low self-esteem, suddenly assumes a role of importance, a part she secretly always wanted. John and Eric immediately respond to Sue's admonitions and the enactment goes into high gear! John then turns to the other players, becoming very moralistic, and reprimands them for not inviting the newcomers into their games.

Discussion and Evaluation

A short discussion will follow in an initial enactment. There may be a problem after the first session because your class is beginning to go out of control. You may have allowed the action to go on too long.

The following guideline may be helpful:

"Allow an enactment to run only until the behavior that is being proposed is clear. Cut the enactment when you have enough data for discussion, or when actors and audience seemed to have gained some insight, or when a skill has been practiced.

Remember that an initial enactment is to help the group to define the situation further, and to identify with the characters; it does not have to be completed to be useful."[4]

Your players have now rejoined the audience. You become a discussion leader. You may ask:

What are the results of what has happened?
How do you all feel?
Can we find another way to solve this problem?

---

[4] Fannie R. Shaftel and George Shaftel, *Role-playing for Social Values* (Englewood Cliffs, New Jersey: Prentice-Hall Inc., 1967), p.97.

Children who come up with alternate solutions may be encouraged to be in subsequent reenactments.

The Reenactment

In the reenactment, two of the children who had isolated themselves in the back of the room now play the roles of the strangers. Perhaps this is an extension of the way they see themselves in the classroom. Other children are now chosen to play the various roles. The reenactment takes a different turn because the children seem more articulate and less excitable. They appear to be more objective about their feelings and what is happening. A new dynamics is taking place with the new players in the roles. The outcome changes.

Other Ways to Present Situations

There are other means for presentation of the problem situation. An effective device is the use of the photograph, which the children look at very briefly and then give their interpretation. Another means is the use of the unfinished story situation. The story is read to the class and the children are given a minute or so to think over what they have heard. Then the story can be reviewed by discussion.

Role-playing activities via many means of presentation are an effective tool of the teacher and counselor.

Summary

Dramatic play, creative dramatics and role-playing are important guidance tools in dealing with all children, the advantaged as well as the disadvantaged, the normal as well as the troubled child.

Pantomime is a good base for creative dramatics. It uses self-expression through body movement and can be referred back to at any age. Dramatic play is free, unorganized and spontaneous. It is a beginning phase in dramatics and is usually used by younger children. In the improvisation of creative dramatics we have spontaneous dialogue in a developed situation. This improvisation can be based on characters, situations, previous pantomime activities, unfinished stories, and original and established plots.

Role-playing or socio-drama is the introduction of the problem situation and the exploration of solutions for the purpose of developing insights into behavior. For all children, creative expression through role-playing is an effective outlet for emotional and social awareness and increased sensitivity to others. In the schools of the disadvantaged, creative dramatics and particularly role-playing helps develop inner discipline through exploration of outcomes of behavior.

Chapter Seven

Class 4-4

About the Monster (Figure 7-1)
by Robert Berman

He is a dragon. His tail looks like a snake winding around. His tongue is red and shoots poyson because he is dangerous. He will eat people alive. He is coming to get me and makes me shiver. I hate him. He looks like Errol and I hate Errol. I would like to punch Errol and the monster.

Guiding Children Through Art Experiences

A class of children looks at a picture of a mythical dragon. It evokes images, fearful and forbidding to some, exciting and romantic to others; it's serpentine shape and verdant coloring become an evocative sensory experience. One little boy draws the story he imagines and writes of it in the lines presented above. Children are being guided by a skillful, imaginative teacher; they are exposed to the visual stimuli of fascinating shapes and motivated into artistic expression.

But art in the elementary school is a neglected area. In a teachers' room one hears:

I certainly will have no art with this class — I'm afraid of losing control. I'll let Betty Calder do it.

There're too many other subjects to worry about.

My whole class did sponge painting and the floor ended up in technicolor and became a skating rink — positively no more art this year. Betty Calder can brave it.

I have art when my venerable supervisor goes out to lunch. He thinks it's a waste of time with a class behind in reading like mine.

101

And finally:

To tell the truth, I can't even draw a box. Who am I to teach art? Miss
Calder has the background.

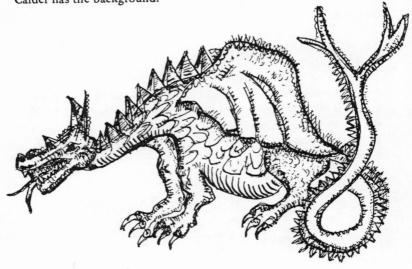

FIGURE 7-1

Art is often looked upon with fear by teachers who may lack
class control, annoyance by those who are pressed hard to teach
the curriculum, and awe by those who lack art ability. All this is
tinged with confusion about the place of art in the curriculum,
varying attitudes of school supervisors toward it, and ever-changing school policies toward this area. In schools where art is given
its proper importance, it is used as an integral and supplementary
activity correlated to subjects such as social studies, reading,
science and music, and for its excellence as a guidance tool for
reaching those "unreachable children." After all, when all else
fails, there's always art.

The Place of Art in Guiding Children

Children's art speaks to us. It is a guidance tool for the
teacher and counselor and can be both diagnostic and therapeutic.
The child who draws himself portrays the person he believes

himself to be, and thus we learn about children through their drawings. Your Errol will draw a picture of himself with sharp teeth to release his aggressive emotions. Jason will paint a fiery, bloody battle in the skies, a leftover residue from a scarred, violent family life. Ellen will use feathery strokes in a timid halting fashion on a drawing paper, sketching in a tiny picture of a girl in a remote corner of the page. Without having even known Ellen and Errol you could contrast the aggressiveness of one and the timidity of the other. (Further in the chapter, we will discuss some diagnostic clues a teacher may use to interpret a child's drawings; but, they should be used with caution.)

Art as a therapeutic tool, providing emotional release, is the approach that you, the teacher, will probably find most useful in the classroom. Artistic expression can uncover and channel anxieties and tensions and aid the child in his classroom functioning.

Using Art in the Classroom

This chapter describes a number of art activities which have been tried and proven effective by teachers themselves. They have been used in bright as well as slow classes, and in classes where there are few disruptive children as well as in classes where there is a preponderance of highly disruptive youngsters. Being a pragmatist, I feel that the most effective means for evaluating what works must come from the teachers themselves. There is no other way.

Miss Calder and Class Management

As indicated in the opening vignette of the chapter, Miss Calder is looked upon as experienced and knowledgeable in art. She is not alone; there are other teachers like her who have done imaginative work with their classes. One watches children in these classes wield assort art materials with zest, order, and a readiness for creativity, but the vehicle by which these experiences take place in good class management in art activities. An interview with Miss Calder, a talented fourth-year teacher, yielded these guidelines for successful art activities.

Do you see guidance principles in class art management? "Definitely! It is better if class management involves planning with the children; they then have a stake in the classroom. We draw up rules together not only in art but in all our activities. The children participate in democratic ways, having a voice; they are learning to develop self-confidence, self-discipline, and self-control. If they do not follow the rules, they know they must assume the consequences. They are learning to work together with commitment."

How do you have such excellent control? "I work at it. I try to be very structured in my planning of the lessons. Remember that I am dealing here with over thirty youngsters, and some very volatile guidance problems. Each lesson is broken down and demonstrated; the children understand what they're to do BEFORE they begin. Gradually, as they progress into the year, the children are given more freedom. This develops naturally."

What about rules? "I believe that the rules formulated and understood by the children themselves have a greater chance of being carried out than those imposed by the teacher. Long lists of rules in the classroom, originated by the teacher and hung up about the room, are of little value.

We discussed the problems of a large class in terms of walking around with paint, etc., and the following rules were decided upon together:

a. Paint monitors and other monitors are selected from each table by the children.
b. Nobody gets out of his seat without permission. This rule is later relaxed when the children are under control.
c. The paint is never taken off the main table except by special paint monitors; I alone dole out the paints. This was my suggestion, and was agreed upon by the class. This rule is never changed and prevents traffic collisions and messy paint accidents.
d. If there are infractions of the rules, the children themselves have decided upon penalties, that is, losing his turn to paint, etc.
e. The children may talk but low enough so that I can be easily heard."
(I find it's natural for children to converse while working. In communication, they learn to assess themselves and release tension.)

About tasks: "In many instances I assign projects to the class, and the children discuss the goals that we want to achieve and tasks we will have to work on in order to achieve those goals."

When do you prepare materials? "I definitely have materials all lined up in advance. The paper for painting is kept on the painting table, as are paint jars, brushes, individual containers for single colors, and ice cube trays for holding several colors. You're courting disaster if you start running around to find things during a painting activity with an entire class on your hands."

What do you paint on? "I have an easel in the back of the room for individual children to paint on, but when the entire class paints, or does other art work, we use the desks. Since we have movable furniture, we place groups of desks together and cover them with old newspapers to keep them clean. The children then have their own cluster of painting buddies. There are generally about five groups of desks placed in a semi-circle about the room, with the main table in the center holding the supplies and paints. The children know *before* they begin moving the desks who their painting buddies are. The movement of desks is accomplished very swiftly, because we had practiced it many times before we even began."

Conclusion: As a conclusion to this interview I watched and participated in a string painting lesson* in Miss Calder's room. She was as good as her words and practiced all the principles she believed in. It was late in the year, and the children were walking freely about bringing finished pictures to the back of the room, and coming up to Miss Calder for fresh paper. There was only one mishap, which was handled goodnaturedly and quickly. The children chatted in a friendly manner; it was an orderly, stimulating, and happy class.

"Learning to Let Go" Is a Beginning!

Remember Aunt Agnes who was overly meticulous and was always cleaning her house? (She was once a little girl who never dirtied her clothes.) We meet children who need to relax (and teachers too) and enjoy themselves by being fully a part of what they do even when it's a bit messy. It's important for the children to learn to "let go" and not be afraid to manipulate materials; allowing children this freedom through art from the early grades on relieves inhibition, exposes them to sensory experiences, and is a forerunner of true artistic expression. They can be fully a part of what they do even when it's a bit messy.

---

*The procedure for this string painting lesson is given at the end of the chapter.

One nice messy activity is sand painting, and the children love it. In one kindergarten classroom children were sprawled all over the floor with their sand paints, pasting and coloring. If you are afraid of eating sand or finding it in your clothing, or have Aunt Agnes for your supervisor, don't try it! However, here is the recipe for sand painting:

1. Take several children to the beach to help you collect several boxes of sand. If you don't feel like going to the beach, substitute cornmeal for sand.
2. After you have survived this experience, gather the following materials: the sand, oaktag or pieces of cardboard, flour and water or glue, and vegetable or food coloring to color the sand. (If using glue, dilute it with water.)
3. Have children make a design on the cardboard, then color the sand, determining what colors to use for the design.
4. Shake off the excess sand. Let the sand painting dry. That's all!

If you are having trouble with custodial help, you may run into difficulty with this activity. One teacher made a trip to the beach and collected the sand only to have it accidentally thrown out from her classroom by the cleanup matron, who understandably stared at it in disbelief!

Motivating for Creative Expression

Teachers have used many means to motivate children creatively. This can be done through exposure of the child to sensory experiences in the environment, reading of poetry, increased aesthetic awareness to visual experiences by prints of pictures, or trips to an art gallery.

One teacher showed a picture of interesting shapes — a dragon, for example. The children drew their own impressions and wrote their individual reactions (story at the beginning of the chapter).

Painting to Music: A provocative way to motivate children into art expression is to use music as a stimulus. In the paintings that result from this experience, it is as if the subconscious of the child were released and borne to the surface of the painting. The following example is based on a combined music-painting lesson observed in a fifth-grade classroom, where children had difficulty in self-expression.

The teacher, Miss Carr, began by playing special, motivating excerpts from Tchaikovsky's *1812 Overture* and Beethoven's *Pastoral Symphony*. The stirring quickening beat of the former record contrasts sharply in feeling with the pastoral quality of the latter.

Children listened attentively to the excerpts from both records. They were then asked to paint their impressions of one selection to which they reacted. A discussion period followed in which the paintings were divided into two groups of moods: paintings of the pastoral or peaceful scenes and paintings of warlike, turbulent scenes. It was interesting to note that most of the boys chose the latter mood, and the girls the peaceful mood. (One can imagine what the Women's Liberation Movement could interpret from this!)

A language arts lesson followed in which the children wrote their reactions (see Chapter Nine, "Using the Sociogram and Other Guidance Techniques.")

In the children's paintings, blues, greens and yellows were used freely in pastoral scenes. In the *1812 Overture* paintings, deep purples, dark greys and black painted somber storm scenes and fiery reds, brilliant yellows and crashing oranges clashed in battle and wreaked turmoil across the painting paper.

Release Through Art in the Classroom

Many teachers use art media to help the children release their tensions. Here are six ideas for using art as a release described by successful teachers:

The Art Corner: "I have a special art corner in my classroom, which is partly secluded by books. We use this corner as a calming down spot, and it is equipped with an assortment of art materials."

The Easel: "Each child has a chance to paint at the easel (Figure 7-2). His or her name is posted on a painting list tacked up in the art corner. However, if a child is particularly upset, I allow him to paint out of turn. It's amazing how the others accept this."

The Art Table: "I have an art table in the back of the room. On it I have a box of all sorts of material, buttons, buckles, glitter, felt, glue and paper. Children can make collages to their hearts' content."

FIGURE 7-2

Use of Clay: "It's marvelous how a child can work out his aggressions and frustrations just pounding on a bit of clay!"

The Bulletin Board: "My bulletin board in the back of the room has a special place on it for art activities. Children have a chance to exhibit their work."

The Mural: "We always have a large class project in art we're engaged in. Now we're making a mosaic fabric mural* about China. I have a very slow class with a short attention span. When the children get extremely restless I have them work on it for a time, and just cutting colorful scraps 'unwinds them' and they are ready to resume academic work."

Observing Children's Behavior in Artwork, or There's One in Every Room!

Children reveal themselves by their gestures and behavior while executing some drawings or painting. How good are you at

---

*Take a piece of muslin and draw an outline for the mural in pencil. Use different shapes of fabric, like a mosaic, to fit the outline.

observing these clues? Some of the children found in every classroom are:

The child who always "messes up" — Johnny is never good enough. He makes three lines on a page and then crumples up his paper. Into the wastebasket it goes, or onto the floor. This child has a low threshold of frustration and impossibly high standards.

The child who never finishes — Walter draws a picture, looks at his neighbor's paper and then puts aside his work and takes another sheet. As far as he's concerned, he's finished! He's a cousin to the child who "messes up."

The child who is always hiding her work — When you pass Nancy's desk, the artwork goes right in the desk. She must be coaxed at the end to relinquish it!

The child who seeks constant approval. "How is *this*, teacher?" and he repeatedly comes up to your desk.

The child who has nervous tics while working and frequently asks to go to the bathroom. (His anxiety is spilling over.)

How many more individual reactions can you notice? They are all clues to the child's emotional development and work hand-in-hand with other criteria for promoting understanding of the child. Severe signs of maladjustment should be referred to the school counselor or psychologist.

Encouraging Every Child

There is nothing really ugly in what the children do in their artwork. But there is a tendency for adults to look at a child's art and comment, "What is it supposed to be?" or, "It doesn't look much like a house." Such comments cause the child to freeze, emotionally speaking. The fact is that a drawing doesn't have to look like a house to be a house. This is the way the child views it. We are somehow tugging at that delicate thread of beginning self-confidence in art when we question in this manner. Of course, one might, after looking at an unaesthetic paper, comment tactfully, "See if you can find new ways, Charles, to make your paper exciting."

But what are we really looking for in a child's art in the elementary grades? Isn't it really to discover whether the child can express himself freely, rather than whether he has good composition and art ability?

There are gifted children who will benefit from supplementary art experiences, but in the classroom, we must encourage every child to give vent to his feelings without inhibition; we must give him a relaxed classroom situation conducive to artistic expression. It's very difficult to be creative in an autocratic setting.

Each child strives hard to create. The pitiful outpourings of some must still be recognized in the light of a total art experience. We have to help each child in the classroom get ready for that next step.

Correlating Art with the Language Arts

A series of painting activities in Miss Calder's room yielded a colorful outpouring of paintings done in different techniques. She then correlated the artwork with written expression. The children's imagination conjured up all sorts of animals, shapes, and happenings, and these were translated into stories. The stories became a vehicle for children's joys, anxieties, and terrors.

For example, Eric wrote the following in response to a string painting which resembled an amusement park (Figure 7-3):

FIGURE 7-3

One day John went to the amusement park with his friends. He rode in little cars and then shot up and down on the roller coaster. It was sometimes scary but exciting! People yelled when they went down the hill. He stood on long lines to get food, and ice cream. You can see long lines in the painting. It was a lot of fun!

Miss Calder had to admit Eric was "a lot of fun" to have in the classroom; cheerful, bright, and always a leader in new projects.

Anthony responded as follows to a wet-string painting*:

All the lines in the painting look like train tracks all jumbled up and there was a terrible accident when the train smashed and lots of blood. Now the painting is turning into a war and a bunch of jets in the sky trailing smoke. The purple line is a plane shot down because there's a big loop of color falling.

Miss Calder discussed Anthony's reaction to the painting with the school psychologist, for Anthony is undergoing psychological evaluation.

In response to a sponge painting,* Karen verbalized a recent trauma of being molested:

A man is going to get a woman. She was screaming very loud. He was taking her away in a car. You shouldn't go in cars with people you don't know.

And last, Timothy, a boy with a perrenial sense of humor, responded to a straw blowing painting* with his typical whimsical outlook toward life. He conveyed his feelings into words in a fable a la Aesop:

"What's up that tree?" the buffalo said, shivering in his buffalo pants. It has many legs and a funny nose. It's a spider! Bless my buffalo heart. It will hop down on my buffalo big fat body and get lost on it. Help! The buffalo ran and ran. The spider laughed because it was so tiny and chased the buffalo away. He laughed a spider's laugh that only another spider can hear and still the buffalo heard it far away.

---

*In a wet-string painting, the paper is wet before the string is applied to achieve an interesting blurred effect. Procedures for sponge painting and straw blowing painting are presented at the end of the chapter.

Guidance Experiences

Art can be used as an integral part of guidance experiences. It can be used to illustrate group writing experiences and in the creation of puppets and their use for dramatic self-expression.

Group Writing

As an outgrowth of a fifth-grade group discussion guidance activity, it was discovered that the children had many conflicts regarding home chores. The class decided to culminate brainstorming activities and class discussion with written expression in the form of solutions to the individual problems in a booklet called "Just Our Gripes." In conjunction with this, the children then illustrated each gripe with humor and surprising talent. The whole booklet was approached in a light vein and at the same time probed for answers to the children's dilemmas.

One gripe concerned the mundane chore of garbage disposal as depicted in Figure 7-4.

Garbage

I am annoyed to have to take the garbage down on chilly nights. I'm in a hurry so I go down without a coat. Brr—brr—

> Signed — "Jerry"
> *Question:*
> What do you do about it?
>
> *Solutions:*
> 1. Take the garbage out on warm nights *or*
> 2. Wear a coat *or*
> 3. Do another chore instead *or*
> 4. Stop complaining!

FIGURE 7-4

Puppetry — Dramatic Self-Expression

No discussion of guidance through art activities would be complete without considering puppetry. Puppetry, a dramatic arts device used effectively in guidance, is also an art medium. A child can assume a new personality using the puppet as a cloak. The child lives the character he portrays and fashions with his hands. Behind this veil the timid child may become the boastful, brash king and the plain child, the dazzling princess. Puppets and their design, then, are an effective means for the transference of feelings, emotions, dreams, and secret wishes. The inanimate puppet becomes another vehicle for the expression of children's feelings.

Younger children enjoy making simple paper-bag puppets, one-string marionettes, and stick puppets. The older child can devise the hand puppet, multi-string marionette, puppets with papier-mache heads, and even pop bottle people. They wear mitten-shaped costumes. One delightful, "gruff old man" was fashioned by a sixth-grade boy out of papier-mache, and a wan old woman was given an ethereal look by a coat of blue paint.

The hand puppet* is not usually attempted until the second grade, but it is this puppet which has been used extensively in hospital therapy because of its close manipulation by the children and contact with the audience. One hand puppet, Casper, was used in Bellevue Hospital in therapeutic puppet shows, and is described here:

> Right from the start we learned that most children identified themselves very closely with Casper. He seemed to express their wishes and desires, and his combination of words with action was a real demonstration for them of how problems could be handled and settled. Casper meets the witch (symbolically the bad mother), the giant (symbolically the bad father), the crocodile (representing oral aggression), and the devil (theological identification). These are symbolic expressions of attitudes and the child himself feels free to project his own attitudes into the show.[1]

Puppetry, then, can be used as therapy in a clinical setting, and as self-expression for the child and guide for the teacher in the classroom. When the child gives life to a puppet and verbally creates and responds to situations, he is providing the teacher with an effective tool for understanding his behavior. Artistically, in the creation of puppet characters, and dramatically in the enacting of their roles, the child reveals himself and provides the teacher with insight into his personality.

Puppetry also offers a good medium for dramatizing social problems and issues. For example, it might be correlated with drug education. Children can be shown the danger of drugs through this medium, for what might be rejected from an adult would be accepted from the mouth of a puppet.

A sixth-grade class wrote an original script for a puppet show about drugs; they devised the puppets and enacted the show in the assembly. The puppets were colored imaginatively, portraying the

---

* Procedures for constructing hand puppets are presented at the end of the chapter.

[1] Adapted from Adolph G. Woltman, "The Use of Puppetry in Therapy," in Nicholas J. Long, William C. Morse, and Ruth G. Newman, *Conflict in the Classroom* (Belmont, Calif.: Wadsworth Publishing Company, Inc.), pp. 206-207. Reprinted from Harold H. Anderson and Charles L. Anderson, *An Introduction to Projective Techniques and Other Devices for Understanding the Dynamics of Human Behavior.* Prentice-Hall, Inc., Englewood Cliffs, N.J.

feelings of the children toward the various characters. For example, dark grey paint was used to color the character of the junkie. In this case, puppetry was a very effective means for guidance in the social context.

Clues to Children's Personality
(Expressive Aspects of Projective Drawings)

One afternoon, Errol drew a picture of himself in your classroom which literally ran off the page. No sheet was large enough for his expansive efforts. He drew with heavy strokes. You looked at the drawing and wondered. What clues to Errol's personality were held on this paper?

As teachers, we are not clinical psychologists doing diagnostic interpretations of children's drawings. We are educators looking at the artwork of children in the hope that it will yield some indicators of personality, so that we can help the child function and more fully understand him. Before making a psychological interpretation it is important to first rule out physiological factors, such as eye disorders, that can cause distortion. The following are some indicators, but should be used with caution and in combination with other criteria. They are based on studies done in the clinical field.

Let's Look At:

(1) **Size of Drawings:** Children like Errol whose drawings are disproportionately large for the page are likely to be aggressive, in contrast to timid Ellen whose tiny figures are hidden in a corner of the drawing sheet. Ellen's work indicates a withdrawn, inhibited child.

Emanuel Hammer cites the following about pressure, stroke, and placement.

(2) **Pressure:** "Children who drew with heavy strokes were generally more assertive than other children. Light strokes were results of either lower energy level or restraint and repression."

(3) **Stroke:** "Children who drew with long strokes stood out for their controlled behavior, whereas children who worked with short strokes showed more impulsive behavior."

(4) **Placement:** "Children who centered their work on the drawing page tended to show more self-directed, self-centered, and more emotional behavior than did the total group. Children who did off-center work tended to show more uncontrolled, dependent qualities."[2]

You might proceed with the four preceding indicators and also note the colors, shapes, and subject matter used repeatedly by the child.

Using Painting As Therapy

In contrast to children painting as an emotional release in a class situation, Miss Kurland, a second grade teacher, uses painting as an outlet for her children in a one-to-one relationship with them. She becomes a kind of therapist during some of her free time when the class has left for another activitity. In the quiet of a classroom without children, a troubled child will remain to paint. She consults with the guidance counselor who employs painting in a similar fashion, and they discuss painting techniques and the guidance aspects of the children involved.

The easel, tempera and finger paints, a supply of brushes, newsprint and fingerpaint paper, an old coffee can to hold brushes, small frozen juice containers to hold paints, and two old men's shirts to be used as smocks are all that are needed. The children do the rest. She keeps a table nearby to accommodate a wet painting while a fresh one is clipped onto the easel. (Children are rarely satisfied with doing one painting.)

Miss Kurland maintains a supply of props in her room, among which are: an odd-shaped free-form sculpture, a pretty blue glass vase and dried orange fall leaves. When the child remains sullen, she speaks to him and something triggers off the painting activity; it usually works! However, when the child is drawn to the easel as a release in the throes of agitation, he seldom needs stimulation, and he knows exactly what he wants to paint; the sheer kinetic sense of pleasure that comes from wielding a wet brush dipped in paint the consistency of sour cream, and onto a surface, streaking

---

[2]Adapted from Emanuel F. Hammer, *The Clinical Application of Projective Drawings* (Springfield, Illinois: courtesy of Charles C. Thomas, Publisher, 1958), pp. 65-69.

it with brilliant colors, is immediate for the child. These feelings can lead to the ultimate satisfaction of creation in a crisis situation.

There are children who paint as though they were pouring their souls on paper. When David in Miss Kurland's class storms about the room after a terrible bout and then executes such a painting, he takes his unaesthetic, muddy looking, violently stroked, paint drenched paper and hands it to her saying, "Here, hang it up." She looks at this outpouring of David and puts it on the table to dry. It is a messy-looking blob! The painting ultimately gets a spot of honor on the wall, a place originally reserved for something more serene. On the bottom of the sheet he has written "David" in a huge scrawl, occupying easily one quarter of the page. When he returns to the classroom after lunch, he grins at his work with satisfaction, saying, "I did that."

If you are a teacher who has not yet experienced the rewards of a one-to-one relationship with a child away from the class situation, this activity is highly rewarding.

Summary

Guidance through art experience in the elementary school is an important medium for children for the free expression of emotion, release of frustration, a growing awareness of self, and emotional growth. It is too frequently overlooked because of the fears of lack of knowledge, skills, and class control, and because of the ambiguous attitudes of the school toward the place of art in the curriculum.

Discussed here are suggestions for art activities in the classroom actually coming from the teachers themselves. Included are suggestions for meaningful class management, motivational activities for creative expression and emotional outlets for art in the classroom.

Art is a vehicle for the expression of children's feelings, and can be used by teachers in conjunction with many other curriculum activities, such as the language arts, dramatic expression and guidance. Clinical psychologists use clues found in projective drawings of children to determine the personality of the child; teachers may use some of these psychological clues to the child's personality.

Try These Art Activities in Your Classroom!

String Painting

Materials: construction or drawing paper
              tempera paint
              pieces of string

Procedure: Dip the string into paint. Move the string about the paper, creating different designs. Repeat the process again using a different string of another color.

For a variation, wet the paper before applying the paint to produce an interesting blurred effect.

String Printing

Materials: construction or drawing paper
              tempera paint
              pieces of string

Procedure: Wet the pieces of string with paint. Place the string in desired patterns on the paper. Fold the paper in half over the string and press down. (This will give you a pattern to keep and a pattern to send home with the child.) Pull out the ends of the extended string. You may now want to begin with another color.

String Collage[3]

Materials: painting paper
              tempera paints
              various lengths of string
              construction paper
              glue
              newspaper

Procedure: Wet the pieces of string in paints of different colors. Then form each piece of painted string into an interesting shape. Let it dry against a sheet of newspaper. (The dried string will maintain its shape.)

---

[3] Adapted from Joyce Novis Laskin, *Arts and Crafts Activities Desk Book* (West Nyack, N.Y.: Parker Publishing Company Inc., 1971), p.227.

Now carefully apply clear-drying glue to the back of each dried string shape. Press it in place on a piece of construction paper, making an attractive abstract arrangement. Let it dry.

Sponge Painting

Materials: sponges in different shapes
tempera paints
various kinds of paper

Procedure: Dip sponges in paint and move them in different ways over the surface of the paper. Use a swirling motion to get varying textured effects. When the paint has dried, the procedure may be repeated with varying colors.

Straw Blowing Painting

Materials: drawing or construction paper
tempera paints
drinking straws cut to desired lengths

Procedure: Place dabs of paint on the paper and blow through the straw onto the paint to make the patterns desired.

FIGURE 7-5

The paint will branch out into irregular patterns. Repeat this procedure in another section of the paper, using the same or a contrasting color.

Constructing a Hand Puppet[4]

Here are directions for making the "Devil" as illustrated in Figure 7-5.

Materials: scraps of cloth
             needle and thread
             scissors
             lightweight cardboard

Procedure: First make the puppet's head and hands. To make the head, stuff a small square of cloth with fabric scraps, and tie it over a tube made of cardboard. This tube should fit snugly over the child's index finger. Facial features may be painted, glued, or sewed to the puppet's head.

To make the puppet's hands, cut two pieces of cloth like mittens and tie them over cardboard tubes. One tube should fit the child's thumb, and the other his middle finger.

The puppet costume is simply a sack-like dress, tied around the puppet's neck, and having holes cut for the hands.[4]

---

[4]Adapted from Mary E. Platts, *Create* (Stevensville, Mich: Educational Service, 1966), p.99.

Chapter Eight

From a Tutor's Log*

Today I help Pedro read. Sometime I get sick of the way he read. He don't know any words like "little" and "house." How come? Maybe if we read together he learn more words. Maybe. I like to teach so I'll come back to this here room tomorrow.

Your teacher,
Carlos Rodriguez

Developing a Guidance-Reading Tutorial Program[1]

Guidance and Academic Needs

If you are a teacher in a middle-class school, your reading problems will not be as acute as those in a school in a slum area and your guidance problems will probably not be as overt in behavior, but they are there nevertheless. In the low socioeconomic areas, the reading-level scores appear to correlate with substandard housing conditions. Lack of adequate diet, of clothing, and of structured family life has spilled over into the classroom, creating patterns of difficulties.

The disruptive child in many cases is the one who has a reading block. If he has a reading block, he lags behind and becomes more disruptive! This child, paradoxically, is not the one who is seen by the corrective reading teacher, in many cases, because he disrupts others in the group. Consequently he can't

---

*From a log of a sixth-grade student in a tutoring program conducted in our school.

[1] This chapter is developed from Elaine T. Koren, "An Experimental Guidance-Reading Program," *The Guidance Clinic* (West Nyack, New York: Parker Publishing Co., Inc., Sept. 1971), p.14.

read and becomes more disruptive! The reading problems and guidance problems often become integral parts of each other.

As a teacher, perhaps like yourself, struggling with children who were poor readers, I became sorely aware of precisely these children who were not getting adequate reading help. There was a need for other programs.

As a counselor, with limited means at the disposal of these children who have both severe psychological and reading disabilities, I felt that some sort of one-to-one relationship had to be established within the school framework. This would take place outside the classroom setting and carry over into the classroom curriculum by acquired skills. What finally evolved was the buddy system, not unique in itself, but one which was to be utilized in a very novel way.

Buddy System and Its Interrelationships

With the cooperation of the principal and guidance-minded supervisors of the grades used and a paraprofessional assigned to guidance, a plan began to take shape. Essentially, it used the services of older children with severe guidance and reading problems as the tutors of younger children with similar problems. The pupils were designated as the tutees. This program was to be under the direction of a teacher-coordinator.

Five of the least promising youngsters from the sixth grade with a potential and talent for highly erratic behavior were elevated to the role of "teachers" (tutors). As soon as the sixth graders entered the pedagogical profession, five youngsters were chosen from the first grade as their pupils (tutees). We held our breath!

Interrelationships slowly, painfully, began to take place. Mistakes were made in matching pupil and "teacher" and the children were rematched when behavioral and personality difficulties became apparent. We finally reached correct buddy situations.

Experience and Change

Tutees: As each day passed, the small first-grade youngsters (all boys) began to look forward eagerly to their sessions with their "big brothers." Two of the small boys who had no fathers or father substitutes in the home began to rely on these older brothers, who were already past age thirteen. One youngster, newly arrived from Puerto Rico, looked up to a sixth-grade Spanish youth for orientation into the new culture. The youngsters even confided their classroom and personal problems to their tutors, and received suprisingly sensible advice. As the teacher-coordinator, it was amusing for me to see the tutors attempt to exert disciplinary action. One very rambunctious youngster of seven was held in place by "Listen, little boy — what are you doin'?" accompanied by the "teacher's" stern look. The tutors were instructed never to hit the youngsters.

Tutors: The sixth-grade boys whose work had been nonexistent in the classroom, and who all had evidenced some kind of emotional block, began to open up and to feel responsibility for "teaching" their younger buddies. They looked forward to the sessions and their classroom teachers noted a greater awareness and interest in the classroom to new reading vocabulary. It was as though they now had a "need" to learn. Simple connectives and pronouns which had been previously stumbled over became an integral tool for other vocabulary.

Evaluation

There are many ways to evaluate a program. From the guidance point of view each child was making a singular relationship, not only with his buddy but also with the other children. All of the children seemed more comfortable and less volatile than they were in the classroom. The fact was that each child was learning at his own rate, feeling the effects of individualized attention. The group had introduced a new atmosphere for learning. It all seemed to make a difference.

Launching Your Program

If you the teacher wish to be a teacher-coordinator, or a participating class teacher for such a program in your school, you may question:

a. What will the program accomplish?
b. What procedures can I follow to establish this program?

The following pages will reflect answers to the preceding two questions. Concerns will be discussed, such as personnel, allotment of time, choice and orientation of the buddies, materials, motivation, independent and group activities, and ways to evaluate your program.

Aims: What Will the Program Accomplish?

The program has the following aims:

1. To improve the self-esteem of the children involved.
2. To improve the learning and reading skills of the buddies:
   a. To improve the reading skills and understanding of the tutor by review and active participation in reading activities.
   b. To improve the reading skills and understanding of the tutee, by one-to-one instruction in vocabulary, phonics and related skills.
3. To help the children make a better psychological adjustment to the class situation.
4. To establish a one-to-one relationship, and because of the "big brother" involvement, become a facility for learning.
5. To provide motivation for both the tutor and tutee in varied reading activities.
6. To provide an emotional outlet for the tutors and tutees by providing varied creative activities.
7. To provide classroom continuity by appropriate planning with classroom teachers.

Program Procedures

Personnel: The following range of adult personnel is needed to effectively launch the program:

1. Teacher-guidance coordinator, who may be a supervisor, teacher, or guidance counselor.
2. Supervisor in charge of the grades used for buddy selection.
3. Guidance counselor, or guidance committee.
4. Classroom teachers of children participating in the program.
5. A guidance assistant, possibly a paraprofessional assigned to guidance.
6. School or district psychologist for consultation purposes.
7. School health services such as a nurse for visual, hearing, and other functional difficulties.
8. School-community psychiatric services, such as clinics, for consultation and treatment of disorders.

In addition, the principal of the school should be apprised of all the developments in this program.

Choosing Buddies: You can probably think of the "famous" youngsters of the school population who have achieved notoriety in direct proportion to a progressive reading disability. As the sixth-year teacher, you may have children who have accumulated a substantial reading loss of at least two years. Many of these children have already been held over for one year somewhere along their career. If you teach in the slums, you may have the dubious honor of having pupils struggling with first and second-grade readers in the sixth year! You may suddenly think, "What can this program possibly accomplish that hasn't already been attempted? These are lost children. Let's face it!"

You are consulted, however, by the supervisor and counselor, and with queasy stomach suggest these doubtful choices in your sixth-grade class as the teachers of the program.

If you are an early grade teacher, you suggest William and Mark, two children from your class with reading and behavioral problems. You might add apologetically that, "It might be difficult for these two to sit still long enough to learn anything."

Yet it's from these ranks that the buddy tutors and tutees are chosen, with the purpose in mind that a one-to-one relationship with each other will become a catalyst for learning.

Screen the Physical Problems First: Children are usually examined each year by the school personnel for visual and auditory defects. The eye charts and the audiometer are usually used for this. However, children in need of glasses and those having a substantial hearing loss often slip through. It is sometimes difficult to differentiate between children who do not pay attention in the classroom and those who simply cannot hear. If the teacher notes that the child does not respond frequently when addressed, this child should be referred to the nurse for appropriate testing. Children chosen for the Guidance-Reading Program should be observed for these possible problems.

As the teacher you probably have identified the child with hearing and vision difficulties, but the brain-damaged child in many instances makes his way through the grades without diagnosis. This brain-injured child is usually a hyperactive, high-strung child with short powers of concentration. You may observe other symptoms of motor uncoordination. Although we are not diagnosticians, children exhibiting such symptoms to a degree out of the ordinary should be referred to the school counselor or psychologist for further neurological testing. It is possible that in diagnosed cases a special class for the brain-injured child may be indicated.

It must be mentioned with a word of caution that many acute anxieties may produce hyperactive symptoms. Even testing by the electroencephalogram (EEG) does not always indicate positive results for brain injury.

A Matter of Space: So after a time, the children have been selected from two grades. The pilot project may start with ten, sixteen, or twenty children, but they all must have a place to meet with room for adequate seating.

Now you look for that meeting place! This is sometimes no easy task in a busy school where space is at a premium. An empty classroom (a precious commodity) or some corner somewhere with a degree of privacy is needed. It should preferably be near the office or room of the coordinating teacher.

Seating Is Important: The use of tables and chairs will facilitate the desired seating of your buddies. Each tutor and tutee should be sitting at an individual table. The proximity of the tutors and the tutees and the close interaction of the coordinating teacher is a key to the development of relationships in the group.

A Matter of Time: A special time should be set aside during the day which would be beneficial to the children involved in terms of the relationship of other class curriculum. (I always felt that the afternoon was a preferable time to meet.)

The pilot group of children should meet a minimum of three times a week for one hour. The fourth meeting would provide for a conference time with the tutors and personnel involved to assess the progress being made.

Size of Group: The pilot group of children would probably not exceed ten, comprising five tutors and five tutees. As the program progresses, more children may be added to the group. However, there should be no more than twenty children meeting at any particular time. It would be preferable to keep the group small to provide for the individual relationships needed. Because of the high distractibility of the children utilized, one must take size into important consideration.

Orientation of Tutors: An orientation period should take place between the tutors for two weeks prior to the launching of the program. This is the time needed to project the tutors into the psychological role of "teachers" and acquaint them with the curriculum of the grade they are tutoring. In one program conducted at the Maimonides Medical Center's learning rehabilitation clinic in New York City, sixth graders were trained to act as teachers. This program is described by Gartner, Kohler, and Riessman in their very excellent book, *Children Teach Children*. Tutors were exposed to a daily, two-week training program. Training involved the learning of highly programmed specific tasks. The tutors became "experts in these tasks, designed to overcome the development problems of the first graders. They also participated in weekly evaluation meetings with the professional teachers. At the end of the school term the sixth-grade tutors helped to select and train fifth graders to take their places the following year."[2]

Materials: Among the many materials that are ready-made or individually constructed by the children themselves are: work folders, scrapbooks, picture dictionaries, logs kept by the tutors, progress charts, experience charts, puppets made and stage sets designed, drawing paper, easel and paints, crayons, clay, old magazines, cards, library books, pocket charts, stories for dramatization, records and record player, reading cards made, rexographed materials, and games and puzzles devised by the buddies.

Activities to Build Motivation

You must remember that the children selected for this program for the most part probably have a lower attention span than their peers, and very often become restless if not adequately

---

[2] Alan Gartner, Mary Kohler and Frank Riessman, *Children Teach Children* (New York: Harper & Row Publishers, 1971), p.45.

motivated. Their restlessness and boredom is part of their general attitude toward reading as an academic activity that bears little significance in their daily lives. An imagination already throttled in many instances by environmental and psychological problems has to be stimulated. This is no easy task! Because the group is small, and should be kept small, trips taken and other techniques for stimulating interest can be more easily handled.

Group Activities

Library Trip: A library trip in and out of the school setting during which the children can browse through books on an individual basis is an excellent experience. Library cards must be obtained and kept by each member of the group. Taking out library books in a public library setting is unfortunately not so simple an experience for a surprisingly large number of children. This lack of awareness of the public library is particularly true in lower socioeconomic areas, where reading matter may be limited in the home.

Library trips within the school setting can be arranged in addition to the regular class library program. Children can be encouraged to engage in independent projects in addition to the classwork. This is particularly beneficial to the tutees of the group.

Role-Playing and Dramatization: This medium, gone into more fully in Chapter Six, is particularly suitable for a group such as this. Development in verbal skills will come through improvisation of simple well-known stories and original material. The role-playing medium is particularly pertinent to reading difficulties, since it involves the use of social problems which are meaningful in terms of children's coping behavior in life situations.

Puppet-Making and Puppet Shows: (See Chapter Seven for more information) Puppet-making is an effective art medium which correlates with the language arts. As in dramatization of any kind, puppetry encourages the development in verbal abilities. The child learns to express himself in complete sentences. The making of the puppets can develop into the presentation of a small puppet show given to a class; it enables the shy child to express himself through the body and voice of the puppet. The puppet becomes his mask to hide behind. Stick figures and stocking puppets will be an effective device for first graders to portray the characters in a story read to the group by the tutors.

Take a Walk! Take a walk with your children. On this walk, words can be gleaned just from simple observations in the neighborhood, and experiences translated on experience charts become a rich language arts experience. It's the highly individual language of these children that we're aiming for here. The children will be taught to be more observant of their environment, and commonly used words take on a new meaning.

Words in parenthesis such as (see) man, (blue) sky, (yellow) sun, (big) house and (little) dog are all part of the Dolch List, a basic sight vocabulary of 220 words that make up 50 to 75 percent of all school reading matter. Many reading manuals contain this list. One such manual is *A Guide for Beginning Teachers of Reading.*[3]

Experience Charts: A chart can be made by the tutors which records the children's experiences collectively or individually. In the group experience, the tutors will elicit the children's reaction to a trip which, for example, the youngsters made together. It can also record personal feelings brought to class as an outgrowth of some individual experience had by one of the children. The group experience chart might read:

```
We took a walk.
We saw a dog.
We were afraid that he would bite.
He barked and ran away.
Where is he now?
```

A personalized chart of a small boy's experience might read:

```
My brother's name is John
I hit him yesterday.
I am sorry.
He is a baby.
```

This personalized chart can be done on paper and either stored in the child's work folder or thrown away. As opposed to

---

[3] *A Guide for the Beginning Teachers of Reading* (New York: Bureau of Curriculum Development, Board of Education, 1967), p.97.

the group experience chart, it belongs to the individual child. The tutors are to help the tutees with the printing of the individual experience chart, under the direction of the teacher-coordinator.

In these charts, the children learn to organize a sequence of ideas and see a concrete recording of orally expressed thoughts. Repetition of words used in the writing of these charts serves to reinforce vocabulary, particularly for the tutors.

Independent and Seatwork Activities

Work Folders: The children keep gaily decorated work folders into which go clippings from magazines, drawings related to stories read and word lists, which are often painstakingly and crudely printed by first graders who have never printed before.

Scrapbooks: Children love to keep scrapbooks. The older tutorial buddies as well as the younger pupils will develop abilities in the classification of objects and organizational skills in their arrangement. This is the time that a full use of the child's interests can come into play. Athletics, racing cars, television performers, musical instruments, rocks, baseball players, animals, singing stars, art appreciation, the circus performers and a list of almost endless possibilities are there to use! (See Figure 8-1.)

FIGURE 8-1

Reading Words and Cutouts: Boxes of ready-made reading words on cards are available, but preferably the tutors should print up reading words for the first-grade tutees. They can be done on small oaktag cards and stored in pocket charts made by the tutors. Games can be played with these cards, and the tutors and tutees can match and identify them.

Clay Modeling: The clay objects which children love to make may be of the simple kind which requires no firing. This is a commercial clay which comes in different colors and has an oil base. It can be used repeatedly.

The early grade children will make things taken from their environment and possibly exhibit them at a display table. Each child brings his own perceptions with him. He is fascinated by a dog, intrigued by a street traffic light, amused by a man with a funny hat, or dismayed by a broken down building in a slum. He will transcribe his feelings into sculpting. After it is done, it can be labeled appropriately and placed on public view.

Power of Music: Music can be a stimulus which evokes word imagery by concepts of slow, fast, and running, in its allegro and andante patterns. Its portrayal of mood, triste, and forte are keyed to the sad and strong passions of childhood. It is an activity which can also be used for a group; it goes hand in hand with art activities and the language arts.

The children can select their own record to listen to at first, perhaps selecting a contemporary piece. In listening to it, you will extract descriptive words and possible situations suggested by the passages. It becomes a powerful stimulus for language arts exploration. These images and situations can be translated into drawings.

It is possible that in listening to music the response may be empty at first. I am reminded of the time when a child in my class opened his eyes and stared blankly after being asked what he saw when he shut his eyes. (The class had been listening to a recording of *Scheherazade*, and had been instructed to close their eyes.) He answered, "I don't see nothing, 'cause when I close my eyes it's dark in here!"

Painting and Drawing: Paintings and drawings used in a scrapbook or set aside for a separate art activity utilize experiences the child has had in an effective way. It is motivation for further learning and therapy for children who enter the group somewhat agitated.

Picture Dictionaries: Of special appeal to children who are beginning to grasp vocabulary and the alphabet, and also the older child who is severely retarded in reading, is the picture dictionary (see Figure 8-2). It is attractive because of its visual appeal to both groups. The children will draw or cut out pictures of objects beginning with the same letter, such as: look, love, late, listen, learn, lady and lemon. The early-grade youngsters will generally alphabetize according to the initial letter of the word; the older child will sophisticatedly attempt the entire word.

FIGURE 8-2

A Treasure Shelf: Children normally bring disassociated objects to the group from time to time. These objects may be tagged by them. For example, a button will be labeled with the appropriate printed word, using both the lower and upper case "Bb" for the initial consonant. These heterogeneous objects may be placed on the "Treasure Shelf" or any other name the shelf may acquire. When there are enough objects placed there, they may be classified.

Evaluation of Your Program

Your program has been under way for a time. How will you know how much progress your children are making in the program? Here are some suggestions for evaluating the effects of the program on the children involved:

1. Once a week, a meeting is to be held between tutors and the teacher-coordinator to assess the program for the tutees.
2. Bi-monthly conferences are to be held between the personnel in the program, such as the classroom teachers, teacher coordinator, assistant principal and guidance counselor, to discuss problems and evaluate progress.
3. Tutors are to evaluate the progress of the tutees (refer to opening note) by keeping logs of their impressions.
4. At the end of the program, the children will be evaluated by classroom teachers and other personnel by:
   a. Development of a one-to-one relationship of the tutor and tutee.
   b. Effect of tutoring sessions on children's classroom functioning.
   c. Acquisition of actual reading skills by tutor and tutee.
   d. Changing attitues toward acceptance of responsibility on the part of the tutor and tutee.
   e. General modification of behavior on the part of the tutor and tutee.

Implications of Program for Future Use and Development

If the program were to be confined entirely to the classroom, a one-to-one relationship would exist in a flexible yet structured learning situation. Five members of a fifth-grade class might be brought in to coach five members of a second-grade class. The climate of the "receiving class" would be an important factor in establishing relationships. The tutors and tutees would have to have a place to work, without distractions, within the class situation. It is obvious that difficulties of distraction, adequate seating and management might present themselves. When working with a number of children, it is best to have the program administered out of the classroom to avoid possible problems inherent in the classroom situation.

Another extension of the program is one where a teacher on his or her "free time" might supervise two children in a tutor-tutee relationship. However, there must be consistency in establishing the time, frequency and children used.

The implications of the program in a broader sense can extend to reach the college-bound high school youngster who is still struggling with reading skills. The high school student, or tutor, can be brought into the elementary school to tutor fourth, fifth, or sixth-grade youngsters and thereby review his own skills. Such a program might be worked out under special government grants.

For those who try the Guidance-Reading Program, it will prove a wonderfully warm and rewarding experience. It affects not only the youngsters involved but all of the personnel who are connected with its inception. It should be considered for future programming. You might try it!

Summary

The Guidance-Reading Program is an experimental approach in dealing with both reading and behavioral problems, which frequently go hand in hand. The program essentially uses the tutorial services of an older group of children (the tutors) in teaching a younger group (the tutees). These children may be selected by the teacher, administrator and counselor, using the services of these three disciplines in close cooperation with one another.

One of the problems of children retarded in reading is motivation. The one-to-one relationship of each child to a buddy, the small size of the group, use of imaginative materials and activities, and the whole individualized appeal of the program serve to motivate the youngsters.

In addition to this, the buddy system and its interrelationships enhances self-esteem, develops responsibility and answers various needs for interpersonal relationships.

This is a program that a teacher can help to initiate in her school as either a participating class teacher or a teacher-coordinator.

Chapter Nine

Ellen-Beth
Class 4-1

I am writing about myself. I am nine years old and have a brother who is eleven. We live in a house on Laurel Street with a dog, my mother and another father. My mother is going to have a baby which is so funny because she is thirty and old. I hope that I get a sister. About my new father.......

(See "Autobiography," p. 142.)

Using the Sociogram and Other Guidance Techniques

A class of 30 sits before you, each child with facets of personality hidden below the surface. How do we uncover the myriad aspects of the child which would enable us to understand and guide him?

Guidance techniques such as the sociogram, autobiography, and language arts media are not new to the classroom; they are described in countless texts. Yet their newness is in their adaptation to your special classroom needs, tailoring them to meet the exigencies of ever-changing classrooms, more in tune to the total functioning of the child. These techniques will give you an effective tool for gaining further insight in the type of planning needed for successful individual and group functioning.

Using the Sociogram

How would our coworkers rate us at work? What is our status in school in relation to other teachers and personnel? Does this idea make you uncomfortable, that possibly we might not be rated as socially desirable as we imagine ourselves to be? Are we isolates, or fringers, or really someone many choose to be with?

The child similarly has a status position in the classroom.

Although you as teacher contribute your share to the social climate of the classroom, the child's position and interrelationship with his peers has a great bearing on his performance. If David, a timid child in class 6-1, has to sit next to Alan, who possesses a swaggering self-confidence, he will be emotionally and academically squelched. An arbitrary seating arrangement based on children's height in line, for example, might produce strange bedfellows. You feel that David would do better if he sat next to William, who is quieter and more supportive than Alan, and as our sociogram will show, better liked.

Class 6-1 and the Sociogram

This is ostensibly a bright, creative group, yet something is wrong. Instead of the class devoting much of its energies to accomplishing its work, the resources of the children have been diverted into settling differences among themselves. The class at times is also apathetic. If you were Mrs. Keller, you would feel the listlessness and lack of spirit of the children. You would see that in one corner of the room several children have formed their own self-sufficient island and stopped communicating with others, and in various positions in the classroom are children who indeed present no overt problems because they are virtually nonexistent.

Why Use the Sociogram? You would like to unite the class, so you have suggested to the group the idea of a class newspaper. The children accept the idea with moderate enthusiasm. You are now concerned that the children participate effectively with one another on the various committees; you decide to administer a sociogram to the class to effect an improved class interaction. In this way you will:

- Pinpoint weaknesses of social interaction in the classroom.
- Effect a better working relationship between members by recognizing their choices.

How Do You Administer the Sociogram? To administer the sociogram, you proceed through these steps:

1. Discuss the reasons and purposes for the sociogram with the class. They should understand exactly why it is being given.
2. Ask all members of the class to "Choose three children from the

class that you would like to work with on a committee for the newspaper."

3. Distribute small sheets of paper or index cards to each child in the class, and instruct each child to write his name on top of the paper and indicate his three choices — 1, 2, 3 — down the page.
4. Stress the confidential nature of each child's answers.

Recording Results: To record results, simply list the *choosers* vertically on a piece of paper and the *chosen* across the top of the paper. Record each child's three choices as shown in Figure 9-1.

This form (Figure 9-1) is the traditional one. However, you might find it unwieldy in handling a class of 30. In a tabulation of a class of 30 or more, you might use an alternate method in order to obviate the necessity of having a large chart to accomodate 30 boxes across the page. This alternate method is shown in Figure 9-2.

Constructing your Sociogram: Follow these steps in constructing the sociogram:

1. Tabulate your scores as in Figure 9-2, adding up the totals. You will find that in the middle grades most of the choices will occur within the same sex.
2. As a guide for positions of children on the sociogram (Figure 9-3), take your highest scorer (here Wendy, with ten choices) and place him or her in the center. Then place the other members at appropriate intervals from the center. The isolates who have no score and the fringers with few choices are at the periphery, and the highest scorers are nearest the center.
3. Use whatever system you want to designate first, second, and third choices (dotted lines, heavy lines, double lines, etc.). Using colored pencils for each choice may prove the simplest system to read.

Here are some things to keep in mind: What kind of stars are the children with highest scores, in this case Wendy and Jason? What does the sociogram look like? Are there a few stars and in-groups, with the remainder of the class off by themselves? What percentage of isolates and fringers are there in relation to the whole class?

One teacher found that her stars were the most disruptive children in the class, and her fringers, the best behaved. She reexamined the value system in the class that brought this about!

CHOOSERS	\\ CHOSEN → MARIA	AMY	JILL	LORI	NANCY	SUSAN	CLAIRE	STACEY	WENDY	BETH	TERRIE	JANIE	ELLEN	SHARI	KEVIN	MICHAEL	ALAN	ERIC	JOHN	ERROL	LEROY	WILLIAM	ROBERT	JASON	MARK	GEORGE	RICHARD	CARLOS	JEFF	DAVE
MARIA				1					3	2																				
AMY			2	3				1																						
JILL				1					2				3																	
LORI			2						1															3						
NANCY	1				3				2																					
SUSAN			2	3							1																			
CLAIRE			3						1																			2		
STACEY	1								2	3																				
WENDY			2	1						3																				
BETH	2			1					3																					
TERRIE			2								1	3																		
JANIE A																														
ELLEN					1				2		3																			
SHARI					1				3	2																				
KEVIN																2		1						3						
MICHAEL																	3							2	1					
ALAN																	3										1	2		
ERIC A																														
JOHN									3										1			2								
ERROL																	3					2					1			
LEROY																								2	3	1				
WILLIAM																	2							1				3		
ROBERT A																														
JASON									3										1			2								
MARK																					1					2	3			
GEORGE																								2	1					3
RICHARD																3	1											2		
CARLOS																	1							3			2			
JEFF																						1		2	3					
DAVE																			1	2				3						
TOTAL CHOICES	2	1	5	5	3	2	0	2	10	2	1	4	2	0	1	4	2	2	1	0	1	6	0	10	3	3	4	4	1	0

A : ABSENT

FIGURE 9-1

Observation and Application: Let's examine the sociogram of class 6-1 and see how it can be utilized. The needs of the class seem to be facilitating better lines of communication and drawing the isolates and fringers into the larger groups.

(a) Wendy and Jason, clearly the stars, can be binding forces used to integrate several of the isolates into their in-groups. Dave and Claire were placed with Wendy and Jason, acknowledging their first choices.

(b) The number of isolates indicates a degree of absence of class spirit.

(c) There are two in-groups, or closed cliques, one composed of Wendy, Lori, Jill, and Janie and the other of Jason, William, and Michael. Although isolates and fringers attempt to get into these groups, there is little reciprocation.

CHOOSER	CHOICES				CHOOSER SELECTED			
	1	2	3		1	2	3	Total
MARIA	NANCY	BETH	WENDY		1	1		2
AMY	STACEY	JILL	LORI		1			1
JILL	LORI	WENDY	JANIE		1	4	1	5
LORI	WENDY	JILL	JASON		2	1	2	5
NANCY	MARIA	BETH	SUSAN		3			3
SUSAN	ELLEN	JILL	LORI		1		1	2
CLAIRE	WENDY	CARLOS	JILL					0
STACEY	AMY	WENDY	TERRIE		1		1	2
WENDY	LORI	JILL	JANIE		2	4	4	10
BETH	NANCY	MARIA	WENDY			2		2
TERRIE	JANIE	LORI	ELLEN				1	1
JANIE A					1		3	4
ELLEN	SUSAN	WENDY	JANIE		1		1	2
SHARI	NANCY	WENDY	STACEY					0
KEVIN	JOHN	MICHAEL	JASON		1			1
MICHAEL	JASON	WILLIAM	ERIC		1	2	1	4
ALAN	RICHARD	CARLOS	WILLIAM		2			2
ERIC A							2	2
JOHN	KEVIN	JASON	WENDY		1			1
ERROL	RICHARD	WILLIAM	ERIC					0
LEROY	GEORGE	JASON	MARK		1			1
WILLIAM	JASON	MICHAEL	RICHARD		1	3	2	6
ROBERT A								0
JASON	MICHAEL	WILLIAM	WENDY		3	4	3	10
MARK	LEROY	GEORGE	CARLOS		1	1	1	3
GEORGE	MARK	JASON	JEFF		1	1	1	3
RICHARD	ALAN	CARLOS	MICHAEL		2	1	1	4
CARLOS	ALAN	RICHARD	JASON			3	1	4
JEFF	WILLIAM	JASON	GEORGE				1	1
DAVE	JASON	MARK	WILLIAM					0

A : ABSENT

FIGURE 9-2

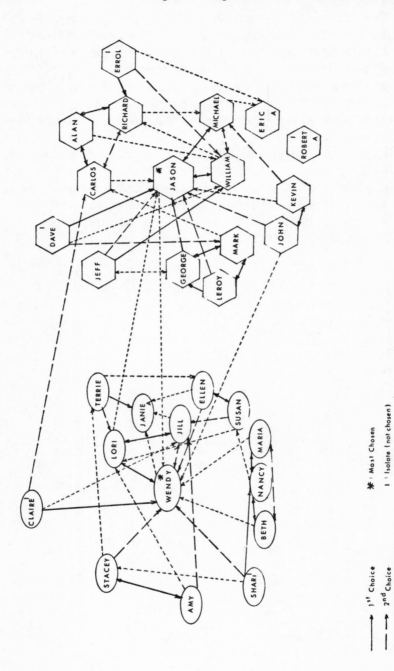

FIGURE 9-3

⟶ : 1ˢᵗ Choice

⟶ : 2ⁿᵈ Choice

- - -▸ : 3ʳᵈ Choice

✱ : Most Chosen

I : Isolate (not chosen)

A : Absent

The fringers Kevin and John (reciprocal choices) are added to the group of Jason, William and Michael. (John has indicated Michael as his second choice.) The group of six now includes David, an isolate. Stacey and Amy (reciprocal choices) are admitted to the girls' in-group based upon Amy's second choice of Jill.

(d) There are separate triangles of boys: Richard, Carlos and Alan, and Mark, Leroy and George; and girls: Nancy, Beth and Maria (reciprocal choices), who operate rather independently of the class. These groups are left intact for the committee work, but the isolates Errol and Shari, who indicate Richard and Nancy as first choices, are admitted to the groups.

Guidance Implications of the Sociogram

The sociogram, in revealing the leaders and isolates, opens up possibilities for the development of more leadership. The fact is that a child is not born to be a leader. He develops leadership as he responds to certain situations. Leadership thus is a result of his actions in a particular setting. Since leadership is the result of a situation, "It is possible for the teacher to arrange situations in which an isolate or near isolate may actually exercise leadership. This is the essence of good guidance."[1]

Every child should have an opportunity to become a leader in some situation. There are many causes for the emergence of isolates. "Many children are isolated because environmental and cultural impoverishment has prevented them from learning certain social skills and conformities. Some boys are isolated because they cannot play catch and throw a ball."[2] Whatever the cause for isolation, these children must be provided with opportunities by you, the teacher, to shine in some situation. The sociogram will be a tool in effecting this individual accomplishment and recognition.

Now Let's Be Realistic! Realistically speaking, a class of 30 makes placement difficult according to choices indicated. The very nature of the tabulation in a class of this size seems enormous to the teacher attempting this for the first time! Don't lose heart, for

---

[1] Roy DeVeri Willey, *Guidance in Elementary Education*, rev. ed. (New York: Harper & Row, Publishers, 1960), p.303.

[2] *Ibid*, p.304.

the next time it will be easier. In some cases, third choices may have to be considered. And some children will not have their choices acknowledged at all! Actual practice, unlike theory, deals with unexpected demands of a classroom; the demands of time, patience, and children's quirks. However, fringers and isolates should be drawn into the group as a priority in placement.

The sociogram is only one of several tools the teacher may use; it is not a panacea for the class's ills, it will not determine the causes for certain behavior, but it certainly provides you with a better understanding of the intricate relationships that exist in the classroom and a better guide for the planning of group work.

So try it!

Additonal Reading: As an additional source, you might consult Helen Hall Jennings, *Sociometry in Group Relations,* revised edition (Washington, D.C.: American Council on Education, 1959) which explores the field of sociometric measurement.

Language Arts Techniques

The Autobiography

Ellen-Beth*
Class 4-1

I am writing about myself. I am nine years old and have a brother who is eleven. We live in a house on Laurel Street with a dog, my mother and another father. My mother is going to have a baby which is so funny because she is thirty and old. I hope that I get a sister. About my new father — I like him and call him daddy. My brother calls him Joe. He is kinda fat and bald on the top of his head and his stomuck sticks out and he smokes a cigar which my mother hates. But he is funny and tells funny jokes. My mother likes him a lot. Last night my other daddy called and there was a fight on the telephone. My mother hates him more than she hates cigars and thats why they're divorced. We sometimes see his other children. I'm glad my mother married again because my brother and I and my mother lived alone in the house before. When I was a little girl, a friend named Susan made fun of me

---

* The Ellen-Beth of this letter is now studying art in a college. Her "new father, Joe" died shortly after this letter was written; however, she got her baby sister.

because daddy left us and I cried. Then her father went and died right in his garage of a heart attack and I guess it was mean of me but I was glad.

I like to play the piano and I am taking lessons. I also like to paint pictures. My new father brought me an easel so I can paint in the family room.

Someday I will go to college and study art or be a teacher like you. Does it take a lot of school to be a teacher? Do you have to be very smart?

I'll tell you some secrets. Sometimes I don't like Joe my new father because he talkes very loud and yells at my brother and when he pinches my cheek it hurts. Sometimes I also cry and I don't know why, just before I go to sleep. I feel better in the morning.

Signed
Ellen-Beth

There is nothing quite as revealing to the teacher as a child's personal account in the form of an autobiography. An autobiography can be directed by the teacher with a prescribed outline — family background, hobbies, and what vocation he chooses. Preferably the unstructured biography is less inhibiting to the child. "The concept behind the unstructured biography is that the pupil will reveal more of himself if he is permitted to write on his own initiative the record of his life's happenings as they occur to him."[3] "The autobiography paints a picture of the feelings and attitudes of the child and will describe ways in which he responds to certain situations more revealingly than, say, through such techniques as the interview or questionnaire."[4]

The preceding autobiography of Ellen-Beth was initiated with suggestions by the teacher as to what to include; the class was then given full reign in self-expression and informed that they might add whatever seemed important to them.

Sentence Completion

Another helpful device for revealing aspects about the child's personality, family relationships, fears, anxieties, and general

[3]Donald G. Mortensen and Allen M. Schmuller, *Guidance in Today's Schools* (New York: John Wiley & Sons, Inc., 1966), p.222.

[4]*Ibid.*, p. 223.

reactions and attitudes is sentence completion. This method provides the child with a part of a sentence and the child supplies his own ending. It is designed to obtain his thoughts on various levels. There are many formal sentence completion tests, but the following responses were collected from children on various grades in answer to incomplete sentences formulated by teachers as an outgrowth of classroom needs.

Response from a third-grade girl:
My greatest wish is...(to have a nice teacher.)

Response from a third-grade boy:
The saddest moment in my life was...(when my grandma died.)

Response from a fifth-grade boy:
I don't like...(girls!)

Response from a fourth-grade girl:
Children don't like me when...(I look pretty.)

Response from a fifth-grade girl:
I am ashamed when...(my father gets drunk.)

Response from a sixth-grade girl:
I am frightened when...(I get a needle.)

Response from a third-grade boy:
Teachers...(shouldn't be so mean.)

Response from a third-grade boy:
I am sad when...(my homework is too hard.)

Response from a sixth-grade girl:
I am tired when... (I have to clean my room.)

Response from a sixth-grade boy:
The worst thing that ever happened was ... (when my dog got ran over.)

Response from a fifth-grade girl:
The best thing that ever happened... (when I had 20 friends at my birthday party and they all brought presents.)

The Story Completion Method

In the Story Completion Method, the child is presented with an unfinished story, usually in the form of a problem to be resolved. The ending then has to be supplied. A similar completion technique can be used for role-playing situations.

This method was tried with a fifth- and sixth-grade class containing a considerable number of children with behavioral difficulties. An unfinished story was completed by a sixth-year girl, who immediately projected herself into the episode, as follows:

> My teacher yelled at Juanita for talking. (The teacher didn't really know it but I was really the one doing the talking. Its just that I don't like to get into trouble in school and I'm always afraid my mother will punish me if I do.)

Here is an unfinished story as it was completed by a fifth-grade boy and girl who had contrasting ideas of morality:

The boy's response

> Jill saw James beating up another boy in the school yard. When James was called to the principal's office, Jill was sent there afterward to tell what she saw. James was her friend. (She didn't want him to get into trouble, so Jill decided not to say anything. Anyway, that makes her a squealer and that's a bad thing.)

The girl's response

> (But Jill knew she had to tell the truth to the principal even if James was her friend. He was wrong to hit another boy.)

As the teacher expected, most of the boys had responses similar to the first completion, and the girls were quite moralistic, siding with the second completion. She wondered what the responses would be if the sexes in the story were reversed. You might try this technique with boys and girls in your class, contrasting both sets of reactions. Note that rationalization may play a great part in the answers.

Picture Association Technique

A child looks at a picture of a woman who is smiling at a young boy. It appears to him that the picture is that of a mother patting her son on the head because he did well on his report card.

The teacher of a class looking at the foregoing tableau is using a method called picture association. It is similar to the projective technique that psychologists use in flashing picture cards and getting children's responses. The child reads into the picture all his feelings, images, and desires. In younger grades, the children may verbalize their responses which the teacher may tabulate; in the older grades, the children will begin to express themselves in composition form on paper. This is another useful technique for gaining increased insight into children.

Other Classroom Revelations from Children*

One sixth-grade teacher of a very gifted class used many means to have children verbally express their innermost feelings and anxieties. In one assignment, the subject of writing about emotions was used as a theme for poetry and prose.

A sixth-grade girl wrote on sadness in a poem entitled, "Tears."

> There are tears in my eyes - my eyes, tears
>   in my eyes.
> My eyes are fighting now but the tears still
>   fall out!
> The world is getting blurry while
> My clothes are getting tear stained.
> The lights are dimmer as my eyes close up
>   with tears.
> Everyone is turning into a giant drop, into
>   puddles of staining.
> I'll sleep but when I wake up all will be dry
>   as a desert.
> But still I'm crying!
> It's not day
> But
> still night!

Another child in the same class wrote this response to the emotion of anger:

> There my dog was lying in the middle of the road, whimpering— All
> bruised from a car which hit him and ran. The neighbors just stared out
> of their little windows, into the middle of the road, doing nothing. The

---

*Four of the members of this unusually bright group came to my office for counseling. The impending adventure of junior high school with all its fears and anxieties left its mark on the group. Although the selections used here do not express this concern, there was a general agitation and restlessness in the class.

heat was terrible and they fanned themselves and clicked their tongues and stared — the poor dog just lay there and waited.

Music Images and Emotions: A fifth-grade class did paintings in response to listening to music (see Chapter Seven) and a language art lesson developed as a result.

Two contrasting pieces of music were listened to by the children; these were the themes from the *1812 Overture* by Tchaikovsky, and the *Pastoral Symphony* by Beethoven. Children's written responses following the painting lesson depicted small vignettes tied in with emotions.

Here are several of their responses to the pastoral theme:

I remember a beautiful country place my family used to go to when my grandmother was alive and I would feed the chickens and two cats. Everyone was happy.

I think of a beautiful house instead of this dirty old building with rats!

and to the *1812 Overture:*

There is a terrible war and people are killing each other!

It makes me think of a lot of yelling and fighting in the streets in the hot summer.

A boy is on drugs and he gets into trouble with the police.

Feelings in Technicolor. A racially mixed second-grade class, who had begun to be aware of ethnic color differences, responded to color feelings. Children were asked to express how a color made them "feel" and "think." Some of their responses follow:

White is ice cream and also snow. My teacher is white, and so are children but its not true because their faces are really pink!

It makes me sad if the blue is very dark. I think it's the night and I don't want to go to sleep and my mother yells at me.

Red is very jolly like Santa Claus's suit, but its scary like blood.

Black is beautiful and you should really like it! I'm black.

You should be careful if you sit on the grass. The green got on my new dress and my mother hollered at me!

I feel good because its sunny and warm. (yellow)

Purple is a bad color!

Summary

Use of guidance techniques in the classroom will help the teacher develop greater insight into class structure and children's feelings and emotions. Consequently, her planning for the class should become more meaningful.

The sociogram in its tabulation of social interaction in the classroom is an effective tool for planning seating, committee work, and activities involving relationships of children one to another. It is a means for integrating those children rejected by the class into the class activities. The sociogram should be used as only one tool of many.

Language arts techniques such as the autobiography, role-playing, sentence completion, story completion, and expression of children through poems and prose reveal personality and emotional aspects of the child.

Chapter Ten

A letter to my teacher
Dear Mr. Richardson,

I wanted to tell you that if I talked more times in the class meetings, they would all fall down dead — the girls I mean. They are jelus because I'm pretty. Today I talked aloud about the topic of having friends and everybodys face — the girls I mean — looked surprised at what I could say and they almost died!

Signed—
A girl in your class
(Don't try to guess who)

Working With Classroom Groups

"Groups" is now the magic word! There are classroom groups, parent groups, children's activity groups, political groups, social groups, action groups, study groups, and community groups. Then one hears of group guidance, group therapy, group counseling, and group dynamics.

Classes are being choked by mounting problems of class management; to apply first aid, individual children are removed from classrooms by guidance personnel to relieve the teacher. But the dam is breaking and individual help administered by these services is inadequate. Counselors take individual children from classrooms, but this hardly makes a ripple in the face of the rising problems of class disruptions. So the counselor works with small groups of children or introduces, as a liaison, activity groups for children, some conducted by hospital workers*, to relieve this

---

*Five such activity groups were introduced into an elementary school. Each group was composed of five members, and met for an hour per week within the school setting. It was conducted by the mental health personnel of Brookdale Hospital in Brooklyn, N.Y.

flood of problems. It is effective, but not enough!

The answer is possibly more in the direction of working with groups within the actual class framework. Guidance personnel such as the counselor and psychologist (and psychiatrist) should be working with the teacher in diagnosis and treatment of class difficulties within the classroom in effecting a more workable situation for management of disruptive children. In addition, the teacher should engage in discussion groups, becoming more skilled in decision-making and problem-solving. Class meetings, as suggested by Glasser (see "Class Meetings," p. 155), can be held on a regular basis to explore and find solutions to problems.

In this chapter, we will speak then of using problem-solving with classroom groups to provide the teacher with guidance tools for smoother class functioning, thereby minimizing class conflict, reducing tensions, and facilitating communication.

The Classroom Group

The group has a common purpose. Well then, you might say, so has a mob. In the mob there is no strengthening of individuals through interaction, rather it requires that its members give up their individuality to an overriding feeling. The mobs which followed Hitler were stirred up by extreme emotions of nationalism and hatred.

The factors that characterize a group are:

The members must be in face-to-face contact with one another.
It must be possible for them to have a high degree of interaction.
They must have some common goal for which they are willing to expend certain energies to reach.[1]

Classroom groups are gathered for a purpose; it is the purpose to learn that differentiates them from other groups. The classroom group is also a group which is required by law. Children are placed in the class quite arbitrarily, and they learn to interact with one another and form friendships. The classroom must become a cocoon for the developing personality of the child.

---

[1] Edward C. Glanz and Robert W. Hayes, *Groups in Guidance* (Boston: Allyn and Bacon, Inc., 1967), p. 6.

Group Interaction

The relationships that children have with each other in a classroom and the way they respond to one another is interaction. In this interaction, behavior is influenced and there may be desirable or undesirable results. In a class where there is turmoil this interaction may be so deleterious as to produce negative influences of one child on another.

Development of Cohesiveness

What is this word that keeps appearing over and over again in relation to groups? Why is it so desirable?

Cohesiveness is a means to an end. It enables the class to learn and work together toward desired goals; it enables the small group to find solutions for its problems. It's a kind of sticking together and is that magic cement without which a group falls apart, fails to act, and its members become indifferent to each other's needs. It is the glue without which a group fails! But attaining cohesiveness is the feat of the teacher.

A Dynamic Group

Your classroom develops a unique personality. The sociogram you have given to your class shows certain relationships of one child to another. Subgroups begin to form within the main group, but this is not static. The children's needs within your classroom make for new subgroupings as different emotional factors come into play. The group is a dynamic, or ever-changing one. The study of group dynamics strives to explore the reasons and effects of this interaction within the group.

Resolving Conflict in Class 6-4

Lets face it, you're the teacher of class 6-4 and your class is a disaster! But after all, the ingredients of this combustible mixture are all there. Half the members of your salty crew come from the ranks of class 5-4 of the preceding year, a group with penchants for pulling fire alarm boxes, urinating in odd places, mysterious disruptions, and, above all, low reading scores. Except for several children, the balance of the class derives its membership from the previous class 5-3, known for its good works and fair reading habits. The year had scarcely begun when a virtual war broke out between the two groups. "I thought I would have half a class to work with, and now I have nothing," you remark to a colleague. "Screaming at them does no good. They're really not bad kids. How can I help them?"

You consult with guidance personnel, who suggest problem-solving.

Problem-Solving Steps

In questions of conflict in the classroom authorities Bany and Johnson advise:

a. Explore the issue, noting points of agreement and disagreement. Write these on the chalkboard.
b. Summarize the disagreements, and explore them further with the class.
c. Help the group define the problem and state it.
d. Ask for solutions and list them.
e. Decide upon the solutions considered best.
f. Get agreement upon the steps needed to carry out the action.[2]

Discussing the Issues

In your class 6-4 you begin group discussion. Through this medium you start to explore the reasons for the conflict between the two groups of children. You initiate the class discussion somewhat fearfully by stating, "It seems as though we have some trouble in this class." Perhaps this was not the correct way to open, you think, but you throw this out to get a reaction, and you do! The enmity of the class erupts into a heated discussion between the adversaries:

"Class 5-3 always got all the commendations* in the assembly and the schoolyard last year. They think they're so good!"

"Yeah, Susan got a service award last year and she's everybody's little darling!" whined Dorothy.

"Yeah," said Charles, "they always laughed when we got yelled at in the assembly."

And then defensive comments from the other group. "We

---

[2]Adapted from Mary A. Baney and Lois V. Johnson, *Classroom Group Behavior* (New York: Macmillan Company, 1964), p. 352.

*Commendation cards are a positive conditioning device to quiet children.

were also yelled at in the hallway when we were noisy and we lost commendations. I don't know why we always have to be picked on by you. We had a 'mean teacher'*   last year and got punished like everybody else when we were bad."

"It's all because we're smarter than you are!"

"Ah you're not so smart, you're pretty dumb," the adversary jeered. Then suddenly, racial feelings emerged:

"I'm going to bring my father up to punch Leroy's father in the nose. He thinks because he's black, he's being picked on." At this onslaught, Leroy shouted back, "Your mother wears cardboard sneakers to church!"

At this point you are thinking of reverting back to more autocratic methods such as bringing in your supervisor to quiet down the class, when suddenly there is a lull. The children, after airing their grievances, seem calmer!

So bravely you say, "We'll continue this discussion tomorrow, but I want you to think about some of the reasons why we are fighting so much in the classroom. In fact, that's your homework assignment. It's not a punishment but something to think about."

"That the homework?" they gleefully echo!

"That's all!" you answer.

During the second session, the racial problem comes up again. "Yeah," said Bill, "the black ones from class 5-4 are causing all the trouble."

"Man, you're no better than us" said Leroy, the leader, "What about the white kids in our bunch? You're picking on them too!"

"You know," said John, "the reason we fight has nothing to do with black and white — maybe some it of — it's really because of unfair things that happened in the assembly last year!"

"What unfair things?" you question.

"Things like 5-3 getting commendations when they weren't even good. We never got anythin'," said Leroy.

"Its true," said John. "We never got nothin'. Its all Mrs.

---

*The connotation of "mean teacher" in children's parylance usually implies a teacher who is strict. When a new teacher is deemed a "mean teacher" by the children, she usually accepts this as a compliment indicating she has control of her class.

Geller's fault — she liked your teacher and that's why, and she didn't like our teacher. She was unfair!"

"Did you deserve the commendations?" you ask?

"We did," John said, "and we got nothin' and we deserved them sometimes. So we decided to be bad because when we were good nobody did nothin'!"

Suddenly the adversary conceded a point! "You know," said Joan, "it's true, Mrs. Geller sometimes gave our class commendations and we didn't even deserve them."

"Its true!" said a few more. "The other class sometimes was good, and deserved them!"

Then you volunteer, "What can we do now? Do you want to spend the rest of the year fighting about something unfair that happened last year?" The class slowly shook their heads. "Let's look at the issues on the board and state the real problem."

Defining the Problem

In the discussion of the points raised, the issues of black against white, smart against dumb, and good children against bad children were discounted as the major problems. The source of the difficulty stemmed from the fact that the children from class 5-4 had been treated unfairly last year and had swiftly gained the reputation as a "dumb and bad class." They wreaked their revenge on the other children.

In subsequent meetings, solutions were arrived at by the children and a plan of action was agreed upon.

Plan of Action

(a) They would work "together" now to capture the assembly and school line-up commendations. The "bad members" incorporated into the class as a whole would have a new status. If they felt they were being unrewarded for their efforts, they would send a delegate to the new assembly leader to explain their case.

(b) They had to be honest about their behavior and not expect rewards they did not earn.

(c) They were to work together on a group arts and crafts project. They decided to sell some of these objects to other classes on the grade.

Results

There was improved behavior as a result of the joint effort of the class. The classroom groups, formerly divided, seemed to merge, reducing much of the tension. In discussing their problems, they had drained off much of the resentment which had accompanied their actions. Although they were not yet paragons of virtue, and were occasionally cited for misbehavior, a certain cohesiveness began to develop between the members of the class, and common goals could be set up.

Read

Definitely consult Mary A. Bany and Lois V. Johnson, *Classroom Group Behavior,* for additional information in group dynamics, such as decision-making. This is an excellent source for the classroom teacher.

Class Meetings[3]

Dr. Glasser, in *Schools Without Failure,* introduces the idea of Class Meetings whereby children have scheduled problem-solving meetings several times a week. These meetings are as essential to the class as an academic subject might be. Although these meetings have some of the ingredients of the problem-solving sessions we discussed, they are more systematized; they deal with problem-solving on a regular basis, rather than spasmodically as the situation arises. These class meetings, initiated in the kindergarten, can continue through the grades, as a regular "diet" of the classroom.

About Reality Therapy

The development of Class Meetings is based on the Reality Therapy philosophy of Dr. Glasser. The basic need of all humans is to love and be loved and develop the sense of self-worth. Through responsible involvement with an adult such as the teacher, Dr. Glasser insists that the child make and honor a commitment to alter his behavior, and be responsible for his own

---

[3]This section is based, with modifications, on the "Class Meetings" as suggested by Dr. William Glasser, *Schools Without Failure* (New York: Harper & Row Publishers, 1969).

actions. This technique encourages children to think critically and solve problems.

Suggestions for Successful Meetings

1. The meetings can at first be demonstrated to classes by a counselor or an administrator, with the teacher eventually assuming the responsiblity for conducting them.
2. Have you and the children sit in a circle.
3. Try to keep the problems discussed on school-based topics. (See "A Teacher Assesses Class Meetings," below.)
4. Start with ten to thirty minutes at the beginning.
5. Try to get all children involved and make a value judgment.
6. Aim to get a commitment for constructive solutions.
7. "Questions should be stimulating and open-ended.
8. "The leader must try not to let children answer merely as they think they should.
9. ` "All replies need be treated with respect and reacted to."[4]
10. The leader must not get the answers from children which may correspond with his own beliefs.

Caution!

   Defer the class meetings if:

There is little teacher control in the classroom.
It is understandable that class meetings, because of the nature of informal discussion, could be difficult at the start with a disorderly class. The children may become completely unmanageable.
Little planning has preceded the meetings.
Classroom meetings take a certain skill and understanding to conduct successfully. They should be carefully planned — often in a team teaching approach — and their objectives must be thoroughly understood.

A Teacher Assesses Class Meetings

   Mr. Richardson, a fifth-grade teacher, and the guidance counselor decided to practice Dr. Glasser's ideas. An interview with Mr. Richardson, with whom these meetings were conducted over a period of a school year, yielded these responses:

---

[4]Adapted from Donald J. O'Donnell and Keith F. Maxwell, "Reality Therapy Works Here," *Instructor* (Instructor Park, Dansville, N.Y.: The Instructor Publications, Inc.), March 1971, Vol. LXXX, No. 7, p. 72.

Why did you have the meetings?

I knew I had a difficult group and I guess being the first one in the school to try them was a little exciting!

How were they initiated?

The counselor demonstrated the meeting for about eight weeks, one session a week, and then I gradually took over.

What topics did you use?

We started out with:

How do you think you get into trouble?
What is a friend?
What do you feel about making fun of people?
Do we need rules, and how do you think they should be made?
What do you do when you are happy, sad, or lonely?
What do you think about playing hookey?
How can we argue without fighting?

(All of the topics selected arose from incidents in the classroom and the needs of children. It was suggested to the teacher that the children write autobiographies of themselves, a guidance technique to be used in conjunction with the class meetings. These autobiographies revealed aspects of loneliness, lack of friendship, and feelings of estrangement and conflict with parents which were used as springboards for class discussion.)

After a while, the children suggested the topics by themselves.

What seating arrangement did you use?

I have very little difficulty in making a large circle in my room since my class is set up in a semi-circle all the time. Incidentally, I find the contact with the teacher is much better when the seating departs from the traditional row approach, and this principle carries over into the class meetings.

Did you encounter any problems?

Definitely. Class size. I found that in practice, if you have more than 20 children in these meetings, you're going to have trouble! I have 30 kids. The counselor took on another fifth-grade group next door with the same register. We both had one session per week. When I had my sessions, Miss Goldsmith's was the receiving class, and drained off about eight kids (allowing for two absences.) With the corresponding few absences in her class, she was not usually saddled with more than 36 children at one time. When she had her meeting, I had crafts or some other prearranged activity with the group. Miss Goldsmith followed the same routine. She and I put two small tables in the back of our rooms to accomodate the extra children. We tried to alternate the children taken out so everyone had a chance at both activities. It worked out pretty well.

Suppose one of you was absent?

I was about to answer that question. If one of us was absent, the meeting was cancelled. I felt that there was more continuity in this than moving the meeting to another day, which would upset scheduled classroom activities. My colleague became so involved in the meetings that she came to school one day with an elevated temperature so as not to disrupt the schedule.

What about discipline?

The children do get noisier than usual, particularly your troublemakers. The problem arises after the meeting in trying to get them back to an academic activity. I stopped fighting that problem and arranged my gym period with the class following the meeting.

I think there's a subtle problem here in discipline because of the ways the kids see you and your change of roles. It feels funny when suddenly you become the all-understanding non-authority figure, no longer giving orders. The children feel this too. You suddenly feel like a guidance counselor. It's not easy to switch back, no matter how permissive you might be as a teacher. Class discussion for a teacher is not easy to come by; it's a hurdle to overcome, because of the teacher image. It's fine when the counselor conducts the meetings, but your role is different in relation to the kids. We as teachers really haven't been prepared for this in our courses; basically, we're only beginning to emerge from the disciplinary methods of the traditional approach. It's going to take time because there's still a lot of confusion about what our role as teachers should be.

Any suggestions?

Definitely have children trained so that they raise their hands to respond, particularly in a large group. Otherwise, everybody talks at once.

What were the children's reactions to the meetings?

The children seemed to realize that any problems they had were not unique. They looked forward to the meetings and were extremely disappointed if a session was missed. They developed a better understanding of themselves and others as time went by.

Fighting in class definitely decreased and I attribute this to the meetings. I feel the meetings drained off some of the antagonisms of the group. There were also fewer verbal disagreements toward the close of the year, which is unusual because this is generally the time of the most friction.

Would you recommend class meetings?

Yes, but as I stated before, I feel the class size is an important factor. Arrangements must be worked out, and at the very least it should be a grade-wide cooperative effort.

Counselor Assesses the Meetings

A district counselor from San Diego, California, used classroom meetings with several classes and offers these suggestions for class management. "It would be helpful for the counselor and the teacher to decide in advance where their limits of tolerance for this kind of free behavior lie. Together they should make clear to the children what is acceptable and where the limits are. Discussion of controls with the students can be helpful, especially if the students set the rules for the meetings themselves."[5]

As a counselor, this writer can see some of the difficulties in class meetings. It still takes considerable skill for both the counselor and teacher to conduct these meetings in problem-solving. There are difficulties also in initiating a program of this sort on a school-wide basis. Glasser speaks of faculty problem-solving. Having sat through countless school faculty meetings which consisted of the distribution of notes at the end of the day, most of us find our questions are often buried in the morass of items presented.

One wonders where problem-solving skills will emerge from; how can we demonstrate them if we do not use them in the

---

[5] Jean P. Malcolm, "Experiences with Class Meetings," *The Guidance Clinic* (West Nyack, New York: Parker Publishing Co., Inc., Dec. 1970), p. 5.

context of the school setting? There is a need for revitalization of the school structure in terms of a more humanistic approach. (See Chapter Fifteen.)

Other Group Guidance Techniques

Communication is essential between the teacher and her class, and among the children with one another. Various techniques can be used in group activities. A sociogram (see Chapter Nine) was used to group children for the production of a class newspaper. This was done strategically, to effect a closer working relationship between the children, use leadership in the class and integrate the "isolates and fringers" into the hub of the activity. After much discussion, six committees were arrived at: art, writing, publicity, bookkeeping, printing, and editorial. The teacher, in order to deal with the monumental task facing the children and with affecting solutions for arising problems, had the children participate in various methods of group interaction.

The Buzz Session

Confronted with the economics of printing the newspaper, the class became divided on questions of the numbers of copies to produce and the charge per copy. The class engaged in buzz sessions; five groups of six children, each formed to discuss the various issues for ten minutes. The teacher circulated among the groups to provide leadership. A child was appointed from each group to record what suggestions the group had come up with and report back to the class. In this way, each member had the courage to contribute in a smaller group, even the fringers and isolates, rather than have several students in the class monopolize the time. (This method might have been used in the preceding section, classroom problem-solving with class 6-4, as a means of discussing an issue).

Role-Playing

The children needed to have the feeling of all working together toward a common goal, creating a newspaper. There was a preponderance of material submitted to the editorial committee. Because of the dictates of space, some of the material could not be used. Hurt feelings and cries of favoritism were directed toward the editorial committee. Suddenly all work was at a standstill.

The teacher initiated a role-playing activity whereby the very children whose work was rejected were cast in the roles of the editorial committee. At the conclusion of several re-enactments, the increased insight into the problems which confronted the editorial committee helped resurrect some of the squelched egos and the work on the newspaper resumed. (See Chapter Six.)

Dramatics

Some of the more histrionic members of the class wrote a one-act dramatization about the workings of a newspaper. Into it poured the humor, stumbling blocks, and uncertainties of six committees interacting in the classroom. The dramatization, which was enacted in the assembly, gave moderately long roles to the class isolates, David and Claire.

The Question Box and Panel Discussion

There was an undercurrent of mixed feelings when the newspaper was begun. The introduction of isolates into the in-groups, fringers into other sub-groups (see "Using the Socio-gram," p.135) put a focus on new relationships which needed to be integrated before the children could proceed with the project at hand. You decide to have children contribute questions anonymously into a question box, exploring solutions for difficulties, and providing an outlet for tensions. Six "experts" including two fringers, Nancy and Jeff, an isolate, Errol, and the in-group members, Wendy, Jason and Lori, served on the panel. (Selections for this panel were suggested by the teacher.) In this way, the leaders of the class initiated the discussions, and the fringers and isolates assumed a new status.

Films and Filmstrips

With the increased influx of minority groups into middle-class white schools, some of the difficulties which children encounter may be racial in origin. The need for increased understanding of the background of the minority child (see Chapter Twelve) may be accomplished by the use of audio-visual media. When the racial problem reared its head in class 6-4, the teacher requested the counselor arrange to show a film depicting a ghetto child and the problems of his environment to the assembly.

She used the film "I Wonder Why," a six-minute gem which won first prize as a U.S. entry in the Children's Film Festival at Cannes. An alternate film, "A Place of My Own," showing the problems of a Spanish girl living in a crowded dwelling, is a theme all children can understand.[6]

Summary

There is a rising trend toward increased involvement with groups. The classroom group has a special significance for the teacher in terms of class management. Guidance techniques of class group discussion aimed at alleviating conflict situations directly in the classroom and enabling children to affect and act on decisions, are an effective means for developing children's self-discipline. Innovative programs such as the "Class Meetings" suggested by Dr. Glasser, held on a regular basis, will enable children to find solutions for individual everyday school problems and promote problem-solving skills.

Other guidance techniques, such as the sociogram (see Chapter Nine), the buzz session, role-playing, dramatics, question box, panel discussions, and the use of films can help the teacher guide and facilitate group work and meaningful interaction.

---

[6]Both films can be obtained from McGraw-Hill Films, West 42nd Street, New York, New York 10036.

Chapter Eleven

Penalties

1. "Playing cards at school (10 lashes)
2. Swearing at school (8 lashes)
3. Drinking liquor at school (8 lashes)
4. Telling lies (7 lashes)
5. Boys and girls playing together (4 lashes)
6. Quarreling (4 lashes)
7. Wearing long fingernails (2 lashes)
8. Blotting one's copybook (2 lashes)
9. Neglecting to bow when going home (2 lashes)"[1]

"Guidance" for behavioral problems
in 1848, in a North Carolina school.

Dealing With Children With Special Behavioral Problems

"Discipline" is the inevitable nemesis of the teaching profession. How many children have you whipped today in your classroom? What has happened is that methods of dealing with problems are changing. When we examine the word "discipline" do we mean external controls or are we, in a more guidance-oriented direction, talking about the development of stronger self-control and maturity? Are we talking about ten lashes (or extra homework) for misbehavior, or about an understanding of how these children with special problems can learn to function in the classroom?

It appears that school misbehaviors have grown worse. If

---

[1] William J. Gnagey, *The Psychology of Discipline in the Classroom* (New York: Macmillan Company, 1968), p.6.

children are not bowing anymore, they may be playing colorful games like "kick the teacher in the shins" or replacing the imbibing of liquor with the sniffing of glue, or, with older children, "shooting up."

Critics of a "permissive" school system cry that discipline has grown lax, for special behavioral problems have become more intense, spilling out into the hallways and producing rampant chaos in some schools. And the burden of maintaining order falls on the classroom teacher. It is you who has to deal with an individual disruptive child in a family or with the seemingly unending progeny of family dynasties* who punctuate your class each year with their severe problems.

So you look for ways to cope with these children:

- You make a study of the kinds of children with special problems you have in your class. You see what works effectively with them.

- You learn some techniques of intervention in order to ward off individual explosions. This is urgent!

- You explore innovative programs such as "Behavior Modification" (positive conditioning or reinforcement).

Working With Behavioral Problems in Class 1-4

"Class 1-4 is a class of little characters!" You've stated this fact many times, and you feel frightfully lucky because they're only first graders. You visualize aggressive Tyrone five years from now! He may be "famous,"** and you breathe a sigh of relief that he is so small now. And then there's hyperactive Jonathan who finds it difficult to stay in his seat or concentrate on anything for any length of time; there's Maria who is so quiet and Jeannie who steals. There's Edward who has tantrums and James who masturbates.

Although youngsters in your class cannot really be stereotyped since behavioral symptoms overlap, certain prominent types of difficulties are manifested in most classrooms. These children

---

*dynasty - This is the author's term for a large hard-core family group of children in the school yielding an unending source of difficulties. When the family moves to another school district, five teachers breathe a collective sigh of relief!

**famous - A term used for a child who is notorious for his acting out behavior.

represent only some of the problems you will encounter. Through identification and understanding of the problems, you may attempt to cope with them.

The Aggressive Child

Identification: One need not go into a long description of the aggressive child who fights, throws objects in anger, and generally disrupts the class. Every teacher has at least one of these children; your child is named Tyrone.

Reason: The overly-aggressive child is basically an insecure child; he is making up for a lack in his life. Once you realize this, it is far easier to "live with him" in the classroom and cope with his behavior. In Tyrone's case he feels he is really not liked by the others so he "throws his weight around" as a compensatory action.

How do you cope?

- Have releases for him in the classroom, for example, the clay, easel, and puppetry discussed in Chapter Seven. These are essential, because he must redirect his energies and release his tensions safely through constructive activities, rather than actions such as pummeling another child.
- Keep him away from another aggressive child. Sometimes a quiet child complements an aggressive one.
- Have him lead one of your projects.
- See the parent and work with her.

Important: Be cautious in doing this! Try to call up a parent at a time other than when the child is in mortal combat. A teacher was shocked to witness a parent dragging her child out of the classroom, beating him with a leather strap. Frequent beatings are often causes for released aggression in the classroom. In this case, the problem was compounded.

- Deflect him with one of the intervention devices when you see him preparing for battle.
- Where does he get into trouble? Is it in the assembly, on line, or in the lunchroom? These are vulnerable areas. Give him something to do at that time.
- Try behavior modification with him (see p.173.)

The Withdrawn Child

The term "withdrawn" can broadly apply to many kinds of behavior, much of it frequently overlooked in the classroom because there is no overt interference with the classwork.

Identification: Maria is a withdrawn child who is very silent, rarely participates in class, and generally keeps away from the other children. These are manifestations of her fears. When she does speak, it's usually in a low whispery tone one can barely hear.

Reason: This condition was partly brought on by her moving from Puerto Rico to this country and into a slum area. Her mother reports that she speaks more freely at home, but in Spanish. She had expressed sadness over leaving her grandmother in Puerto Rico, and is finding the readjustment difficult.

How do you cope?

- Gently encourage her to contribute in class, but do not pressure her.
- Introduce puppetry as a medium for her to express herself, for the puppet can become a cloak to hide her fears.
- Try to place her next to a child whom she may indicate a preference to be with. (See "Using the Sociogram," p.135.) Try to have her develop a friendship.
- Give her work which will raise her self-esteem.
- Your relationship with this child is paramount because she is reacting to a loss of security. Take a few moments out of the day to acknowledge her in some way.
- Refer her to the school counselor if the situation shows little improvement.
- Try behavior modification with her.

The Hyperactive Child

Identification: Jonathan has been classified by psychological testing as hyperactive. He is extremely restless most of the time, has a short attention span, and seems to be everywhere at once. He is easy to spot because he is always picking at something — his nose, his hair, his chin, or his pencil. He keeps leaving the room on any pretext.

Reason: There are many possible reasons for this nervous behavior, including high expectations from his parents, lack of personal achievement, pushing too hard, or minimal brain dysfunction. (Neurological tests indicating the last may call for his placement in a special class.)

How do you cope?

- Show him that you like him and what he is doing. (You can pass his desk while he is working and give him special encouragement.)
- Do not seat him near excitable children. They will agitate him even more. Place him near a quiet and level-headed peer.
- Provide acceptable outlets for his tension. Give him several single tasks to finish instead of one long one. Give him monitorial assignments.
- Try behavior modification with him.

The Child Nobody Likes

Julia has been identified by your sociogram as an isolate. When the children whispered their choices for buddies they selected to sit near, one child added emphatically, "But *not* Julia!" For Julia has the capacity for turning any child against her within a space of ten minutes. Inevitably she will turn the whole class against her. Her talent for this is quite remarkable, but she pays the price in frustration.

Reason: Class isolates may be relatively pleasant children with some social lack, such as Maria. The child nobody likes is a youngster with few redeeming social features. Somewhere along the line, Julia has been shut out; somewhere she learned that by demeaning others, instigating little plots, pitting one group against another, and trying to gain control by devious means, she can manipulate the environment and make her presence felt.

How do you cope?

How do you stop children from kicking such a child on line as they pass her, or from sticking out their tongues when they pass her desk? You will have to ignore a great deal of this; it is not an easy problem to handle because a great number of children are involved.

- You might refer her to the guidance services, where she is put into small group therapy to facilitate her interaction with others. However, her progress is erratic.
- Where do you seat her. You try her near a small group of

sympathetic quiet girls, and know that based on past experience, frequent changes of seating are a necessity.

- You give her special jobs to give her the attention she craves, but this must be done with extreme caution so that the others are not antagonized.
- You have, when possible, short discussions with her to try to establish rapport.
- And, you try to like her. This may be most difficult to do, especially after she comments, "You're funny looking, teacher!" Be patient!

The Child Who Steals

Identification: Pens, pencils, crayons, paper from the closet, children's lunch money tied up in small handkerchiefs; all these mysteriously disappear. You look for the culprit and everyone becomes suspicious. A girl cries that her new pen has disappeared; a boy points the finger at someone and there is a hot denial. Two boys turn their pockets inside out to prove their innocence without being asked. In two weeks a host of things are gone, you are at the end of your rope, and then you notice her. Jeannie is furtively slipping Barbara's new notebook into her school bag. You watch her closely as she adds John's nickel from his desk to her booty.

Reason: There are many causes for stealing and other types of dishonesty. These are just symptoms. Feelings of inadequacy, bids for attention and economic deprivation may be some. Kleptomania may be insipient and needing attention. Petty thievery is not unusual in children. Mothers have frequently admitted to teachers and counselors that their children have taken things from their purses; some of these children are crying out for limits, controls and supervision which may be inadequate. Some are trying to fill in the gaps of affection with objects. Whatever the causes, they should be ascertained and dealt with.

How do you cope?

- Use stealing or another case of dishonesty as a good opportunity for group guidance lessons on honesty. In this way, you will not be singling out individual children and will help to establish values and codes of behavior for everyone in the class. A topic for a lesson might be, "How to Respect Each Other's Belongings."
- Definitely speak and work with the parent in resolving difficulties.

- Remove objects that would tempt the child.
- Sit the child in a place which is in full view of your desk.
- Don't spotlight the child; rather, speak to her quietly about the problem.
- If the problem is severe, consult the counselor.

Temper Tantrums

In the early grades temper tantrums are fairly common. There are few things more disconcerting to a teacher than:

Identification: Edward, who screams hysterically, fights with all who approach him, kicks his arms and legs and frequently throws himself to the floor when thwarted in any way.

Reason: When a tantrum occurs, it is as though the pot has boiled over. Certainly, you feel tantrums should have outlived their usefulness by age three, but they continue. Improper handling of these tantrums at home fosters a child's attention-getting technique, which he hangs onto because it works. Sometimes, fatigue and an inability to deal adequately with frustration of any sort are reasons for tantrums to continue till school age. (Tantrums are carried into adulthood in different forms.)

How do you cope?
- First, stay calm!
- Try to distract him, but if the situation becomes worse remove the child to a quiet spot in another room and then go about your business, showing him you are unmoved by the tantrum. If he does not receive the attention he seeks, he will have to find another way to resolve his difficulties.
- After the tantrum thrower has sat in another room for a time to "cool off," you might give him a face-saving activity by suggesting something new for him to do. (This will enable him to assess the impact of his tantrum.)
- If you see Edward on the verge of another tantrum, practice signal interference and see if you can reward alternative behavior. (See "Behavior Modification," p.173.)

Masturbation

You are a new teacher and masturbation in your classroom was one behavioral problem you didn't count on! It certainly wasn't mentioned in any of your teaching manuals.

Identification: A boy, James, suddenly attracts your eyes during a math lesson because he is fooling with something under the desk. You are puzzled by the odd expression on his face, and you walk toward him. Observing him playing with his genitals comes as a surprise. James now sees you staring at him so he stops what he's doing and looks guilty. You pause, and then go on with the lesson. But it happens again. You don't know quite how to handle the situation and this time James seems unaware that you are watching him.

Reason: Children masturbate for a variety of reasons. One reason may be clothing that is too tight for the body. Some children handle their genitals when they have to urinate and many because they find masturbation pleasurable. In James' case, it's a manifestation of nervousness.

How Do You Cope? Strangely, at this point much of the problem may be your own, particularly if you are unduly shocked. There is nothing terrible about masturbation, however, after the age of six, there is an effort to control it on the child's part. It is at this point that you must exercise judgement as to what action to take.

- Don't call the child's attention to the masturbation publicly, although you feel it should be discouraged in a social situation.
- If the masturbation is infrequent, it might be ignored completely; calling attention to it will reinforce it.
- If masturbation continues for any length of time, try to divert the child by, "James, how would you like to deliver this note to Miss Calder for me?"
- If the masturbation appears excessive, you might consult with the parents for further help.
- If the child shows high-strung nervous tendencies, you should refer the child to the counselor or psychologist for further screening. The masturbation is just a symptom, usually done absent-mindedly when the child is preoccupied.

Methods of Intervention

Fritz Redl suggests a number of techniques to use with the aggressive child which may be applied to a number of other behavioral problems in the classroom. Four techniques will be discussed here: planned ignoring, signal interference, humor, and hurdle-help.[2] They were selected for getting you over the "rough spots" of managing surface behavior

Planned Ignoring

Children use all sorts of devices to get your attention. Each time you call attention to them, you are reinforcing the misbehavior. "As long as this behavior is within the range of tolerability, and as long as contagion initiation for others can be halfway kept in check, 'ignoring' leads to faster stoppage, at less expense, than interference would."[3] Then, you ask, "What happened to the advice we all got as new teachers about not letting the child get away with a thing! If we allow the child one inch of territory, he'll take over the classroom entirely with his antics." That advice we received worked for some of us, but it did not eradicate the misbehavior. Those who were strong held the monstrous "recalcitrant" at bay, but one false move and he descended upon us. Some of this misbehavior can die out quickly under planned ignoring.

Signal Interference

Do you remember when your teacher would give you a funny look and you would stop frozen at whatever you were doing? This technique can be applied systematically by teachers using all sorts of signals to indicate to the child to "watch out" and control himself. A whole variety of signals can be used to indicate disapproval, such as eye movements, coughing, facial expressions, and hand gestures. To be most effective, the signal interference should be used in the early stage of the misbehavior.

Tension Decontamination Through Humor

A teacher laughs, a class laughs, and tension is reduced in what might have been a situation fraught with potential difficulty. This writer feels that a sense of humor is much like having money. If you have it, then you can use it. Perhaps when we talk about keeping one's sense of humor, we really mean keeping one's perspective about what happens in the classroom. We sometimes

---

[2]Adapted from Fritz Redl and David Wineman, *Controls From Within* (Glencoe, Illinois: The Free Press, 1952), pp. 158-175.

[3]*Ibid.*, p. 159.

forget, as educators, that we are dealing with young children. One teacher was puzzled as to why the same children always appeared smaller outside of school than they did in the classroom. Do our perceptions become warped?

The teacher's outlook on children colors her relationship with them. Some teachers are afraid of losing control if they see humor in tense classroom situations and make light of them to the children. Yet it often works the other way.

The author walked past a room one afternoon and saw bedlam raging; three fights were progressing simultaneously in a second-grade class where a substitute teacher was struggling to keep order. "I'll bet I can have the class in their seats in one minute by just tweaking my nose," I said. One girl shouted, "She's a witch," and the children suddenly quieted down and began to file into their seats with great interest. "I can make you all disappear if I choose, especially the children who are fighting." The children began to grin, then chuckle, and then laugh aloud.

One child said in earnest, "Make Eric disappear and don't bring him back." She was making use of my yet unproven talents. This was a kind of unorthodox guidance, and I made a hasty retreat lest my abilities be challenged. The substitute reported that the class seemed to be more relaxed after this episode, though still very noisy. However, they stopped fighting. The class's anxiety over the teacher's absence had vanished! (Sorcery may become an additional requirement of the guidance department.)*

Hurdle-Help

The path of the disadvantaged child and the slow child is strewn with hurdles. In fact, this kind of child may never get over the very first obstacles, and consequently he sinks into an abyss of confusion and mounting misbehavior. Your pacing may be too quick for some children or your assignments not explicit enough. The child, rather than revealing his academic inadequacies, diverts his energies elsewhere and starts acting up. He needs help to surmount this hurdle. Being able to detect it will prevent further misbehavior.

---

*At the end of the year, this same second-grade class passed my office door, and I heard a child exclaim in a loud voice, "A funny witch lives in there!"

Behavior Modification with Class 1-4

You have tried to identify disruptive behavior. You can deal with it in the classroom by attempting to actually modify that behavior by a planned program of reinforcement. This is a behavioral approach, experimental in nature, and will take patience, but you can initiate a pilot program for this in your school. Before making the attempt, consult with the school counselor and psychologist for additional suggestions.

What Is Behavior Modification?

This is a system of identifying behavior patterns that require change and affecting conditions to produce the needed change. It is based on the operant conditioning principles (also known as reinforcement) of B.F. Skinner. The premise is that behavior which is positively reinforced will repeat itself, behavior which is negatively reinforced will be suppressed, and behavior which is not reinforced will disappear. Working on this premise, you the teacher have the power to "shape" the behavior that you want reinforced.

There is much behavior which, by punishment, we are actually rewarding and positively conditioning.

A Classroom Guide for Behavior Modification

Suppose we start with the children of your first-year class whom we discussed earlier.

Tyrone, your aggressive child, strikes out at other boys.

Jonathan, the hyperactive one, jumps constantly out of his seat.

Maria barely speaks.

Start on a limited basis with one or two children. Follow through on this behavior.

(1) *Identify* the behavior you want to eliminate. Let's take Jonathan who keeps popping out of his seat, and Tyrone who hits others. Remember that you try to eliminate one behavior at a time, otherwise things will become confused.

(2) *Record* the number of times he does this, for example, 20 minutes a day for three days to a week. Does he do this 5, 10, 15 times? You are going to compare this figure later with results you

obtain with the positive conditioning. You may make a behavioral record chart or simply take notes.

(3) *Reinforcement Period* begins! Here you give the child a reward for behavior you want brought out.

(a) The first thing that you must remember is that you are going to *ignore* undesirable behavior. This is not easy to do! Usually when a child acts inappropriately, you reprove his behavior with, "Jonathan, stay in your seat!" or "Tyrone, stop fighting!" By doing this countless times a week you may actually be reinforcing the kind of behavior you want to eliminate by giving the child the attention he desires. The temptation to call attention to it will be there. (Of course, if Tyrone's behavior is threatening the safety of another child, you must stop it.)

(b) If you are going to ignore negative behavior, then you must *reward* positive behavior. In the case of Jonathan, who keeps popping out of his seat, you must reward him for the times he *remains* in his seat. In the case of Tyrone, who fights with other children, you reward him for *taking other action* as a means of settling his differences.

(c) *Rewards* can be primary reinforcers such as toys, gifts, stars, tokens and money, and secondary reinforcers such as approval, praise, attention, and a pat on the head. The aim is to go from primary to secondary reinforcement, to instill self-discipline. You may use a token to represent a period of time. For example, if Jonathan sits in his seat for 30 minutes, he gets a glittering star. Eventually these tokens are accumulated and a prize or reward is given for a specified number.

(4) *Stop Reinforcement!* How can you be sure now of what's causing the improvements? Jonathan hasn't been getting much sleep and seems more docile in class. Is his improvement perhaps accidental? "To check these possibilities, discontinue the application of the specific reinforcement for a short period of time. When this is done undesirable behavior usually increases and desirable behavior decreases. Now you will know for sure whether or not the reinforcement program was effective."[3]

(5) *Reinforce Again!* Resume the reinforcements once again

---

[3] Irwin G. Sarason, Edward M. Glaser, George A. Fargo, *Reinforcing Productive Classroom Behavior: A Teacher's Guide to Behavior Modification* (New York: Behavioral Publications, 1972), p. 17.

and watch the positive behavior increase. Record results and compare the number of responses before the reinforcement period, during discontinuance and after resumption.

You've Done It!

Continue and follow through. Now expand. After rewarding Jonathan for staying in his seat and Tyrone for finding other more verbal means for settling his fights, you might try rewarding Maria for contributing in class discussions. Care must be taken not to embarrass her with undue attention. This is precisely one of the things she is afraid of.

But Remember!

1. *Consult* with the counselor or psychologist if attempting behavior modification with a child who is under psychiatric treatment.
2. *Is* the behavior you are extinguishing too general in nature?
3. Start *simply* with a relatively easy behavior to extinguish.
4. *Use* other personnel in the school for advice, such as the counselor and psychologist.
5. *Pinpoint* the correct behavior to extinguish first. (The one you are choosing may be linked to another which should be eliminated first.)
6. *Don't* be discouraged if you notice a worsening of behavior. Ignoring of undesirable behavior may be quite upsetting to the child who expects a reaction from you. "Bug the teacher," for example, is a common game which brings a perverse kind of satisfaction to the child. When you interfere with the stimulus-response by not reacting, the child may renew his efforts in full measure. This is not the time for you to abandon your efforts! Stick to your guns until the child realizes that he must find another way to act.

Approaches for the Classroom

You may reward a whole class for productive behavior. Of course in this case you must establish what goals you want, for example, to work quietly, pay attention, etc., and they must participate and understand the setting up of these goals.

In one class, the teacher rewarded productive behavior with a token economy. It was effected this way: "The child worked on the assigned problems, after which he was instructed to go directly to the teacher. He earned points (tokens) in proportion to the quality of his work. The points had reinforcing value according to a formal economic system. Ten points earned participating in recess activities; twenty points earned either a double length recess, or if the pupil preferred, the opportunity to feed three caged animals in the classroom."[4]

Teachers, Counselors and Parents in Supportive Roles

The system of behavior modification has been used not only in schools but also in hospitals. At the Community Health Clinic of Maimonides Hospital in Brooklyn, New York, a behavioral therapist described a group of disturbed youngsters who were unable to sit together for more than five to ten minutes at a time. By issuing tokens representing periods of time, the youngsters were able to prolong their sitting time for longer periods.*

A child who is driving the teacher "up a wall" is in many instances doing the same to the parent. Let's take the case of Bruce, a twelve-year-old, who was brought into Maimonides Health Clinic by his mother; she was motivated to do so by the school guidance counselor, who submitted a full report to the therapist. Bruce exhibited behavior such as bullying, lying, cheating, and bed-wetting. In this instance the mother was employed as a co-therapist. The aim was to provide therapy for an ineffective and immature mother as well as the child, so that the mother's role as co-therapist was central to the dynamics of the interaction.**

Through the therapist's discussion with Bruce as to reasons for his feelings and behavior, and through discussions with the mother as to the ambivalence of her feelings and handling of her son, insight was developed on the part of the mother and son, motivating them to self-change. A reward system of reinforcements was set up in a structured situation with limits set, helping Bruce switch from negative to positive behavior. The mother was to provide him with tokens which represented positive action. When the required number were saved, he would get an English racer.

The attitudinal change in Bruce was reflected in the classroom as well as the home, where he replaced acting out

---

[4] Sarason, Glaser and Fargo, *Reinforcing Productive Classroom Behavior*, p.32.

*Based on a personal interview with the behavioral therapist.

**Based on a personal communication with Dr. Cecilia Pollack.

behavior toward other children with more positive action.[5]

In cases of school phobias, aggressiveness in the classroom, motivational problems, etc., the therapist works very closely with the teacher, counselor, and parents as co-therapists. There must be close interaction between all playing a part in the child's progress. Adequate feedback, frequently a weakness in school-hospital communication, must be effected between teacher, counselor, parent, and therapist, if adequate follow-through is to be reflected in the classroom.

Summary

This chapter details three approaches for dealing with special behavioral problems in the classroom:

1. Identification, understanding and coping techniques.
2. Intervention devices.
3. Experimental approach — behavior modification.

Different types of children with behavioral problems are discussed: the aggressive, withdrawn, hyperactive, the child nobody likes, the child who steals, the child with temper tantrums and the child who masturbates. Suggestions are offered for ways to cope with this behavior in the classroom.

Several intervention devices are suggested to ward off potentially explosive behavior such as planned ignoring, signal interference, and the use of humor.

Experimental behavioral techniques such as behavior modification (or reinforcement) may be used by the teacher for the reinforcement of desirable behavior and the eradication of undesirable actions. This behavior modification is not only used in the classroom but in the hospitals as well by behavior therapists. The parent, teacher and counselor, in many instances, act as co-therapists.

---

[5] Adapted from Cecilia Pollack, "Behavior Therapy with Predelinquent Boy of Twelve," *Advances in Behavior Therapy* (New York: Academic Press, 1972), pp.7-12.

Chapter Twelve

One comes up through years in the ghetto feeling the souls of children and teachers who struggle together for existence day after day. In this, we find some of the answers that make for survival. There are teachers and children who make it and those who don't, and when one wonders what makes the difference, it is, undoubtedly, attitude.

Guidance in the Ghetto

An ambulance screams its way down a ghetto street littered with broken bottles, decaying frames of buildings rotting away, and makes its way through a Brownsville slum in Brooklyn to fetch a small boy whose abdomen is swollen from sickle cell anemia. It stops in front of an elementary school built not long after the turn of the century and takes the boy on to a local hospital.

If the ghetto breeds despair, it is also struggling to rise from its ashes with the hopes for a new future for its children, a new future arising from a more relevant curriculum, more teacher understanding, and a changing social structure. It is in the ghetto classroom that many a new teacher fresh from college courses cuts her eyeteeth, and it is here that she is often hit with a case of cultural shock and disbelief in her first year. It is here that she sometimes falters and resigns; for of all of the paradoxes by far the greatest is the placement of inexperienced teachers in schools which demand the ultimate in professionalism and competency. But perhaps the real paradox is that these new teachers can attempt to meet this situation with a fresher and more idealistic approach.

The author's attempt in this chapter is to probe into the feelings of the ghetto child and the ghetto teacher. Through years of personal experience in the ghetto neighborhoods, one comes up not with cookbook recipes for the classroom, but a feeling for the souls of the children and teachers who struggle together for existence day after day. In this we find some of the answers that make for survival. There are teachers and children who do make it and those who don't, and when one wonders what makes the difference, it is, undoubtedly, attitude.

The Ghetto Child — A Closer Look

When we speak of the ghetto child, we usually think of the culturally disadvantaged, or the minority child. In this Brooklyn slum of Brownsville, for example, it is chiefly black with a smaller percentage of Puerto Rican families.

You are a new teacher. You face the ghetto child each day and see that his background is not the same as your own. You're surprised that he may have four brothers, three of whom have different surnames. You're angry that Mrs. Williams sent her son to school with such a dirty shirt on and you would like to ship him home; you can't understand why so many of the children are so slow in reading and why so many seem so disinterested. You wonder why they are so quick to disorder and so defiant of authority. So you open your eyes and begin to ask questions. What is the child you teach really like?

You see that he frequently lives in a shabby apartment, or in an old two-family home. The rent in many instances is paid by the Department of Social Services (Welfare). You find that Social Services has an important role in the lives of these people since it doles out the clothing, food, and rent allowances.

Your children often come to school shabby. One child wears a polo shirt over a pajama top; occasionally he is sleepy, he has spent his night in a hallway, or shared his bed with two younger brothers; or smelly, he has the odor of a urine-stained mattress in his clothing; or agitated, his baby sister has been taken to the hospital because of a rat bite.

His speech is colorful, explicit, and uninhibited. "This ain't no Welfare shirt, don't touch it!" he says in anger as you try to put him in his seat; or "You're momma eats welfare meat!" one child ranks out another. "Welfare" is a magic word of condemnation! And then, so is "Momma." One child ranks superlatively, "Your momma sits under the sewer with rats and her whole generation!"

And this can't be real! Sex rears its head in the strangest ways. Eight-year-olds in your second-grade describe sexual intercourse in an alleyway without fully comprehending the implications. Words become forbidden to mention; even a combination like pussy willow, introduced innocently by you during a test, is met with an uproar. You take care not to mention the word pussy again even in relation to a cat!

Then there is the literati of the slum who produced poetry like this living sonnet to New York City:

I saw you in
Sewer seven
Pipe eleven
Cage two
Bronx Zoo

And the speech patterns sound different. You hear "she be," or "he bad," or "he do," or "they was." Verbs are omitted and subjects and verbs do not agree. You wonder about how much correcting of this speech you should do.

And then there are the latch-key children who sit in every class with a key on a string about their necks, letting themselves in at three o'clock to loneliness and lack of supervision; or who are minded by a big sister who has taken off from high school to watch a brood of youngsters while the mother is working. The latch-key children are swelling in numbers as more opportunities are created for the mother through the community and federally funded training programs. A black middle-class group of women is emerging, leaving the men behind. And with the working mother, the social issues arise: a desperate need for child-care centers to free the family from the Welfare roles, so that big sister will not have to lose time from high school to watch the young.

Prejudice and hostility exists; the white teacher is regarded as the interloper. It comes out in different forms. The child is angry. You touch him and he retorts, "Get your white hands off me!" or "You white bitch teacher!" Anti-Semitism has reared its head in the ghetto where a large proportion of teachers are Jewish. "She's a Jew teacher," said one child. "No she ain't, she's too nice," answered another.

The ghetto child grows up in all of this and survives. The boy without a father searches desperately for a male teacher to identify with and finds few images. The small girl looks for security and warmth in the classroom and she is frequently too slow and confused about the directions the teacher gives. This is the ghetto child, the child you must teach. Those teachers who lack some identification with the underdog will have a more difficult time of it; those whose expectations are too high or not high enough will miss the mark, for what is most important are basic attitudes.

Teaching Problems in the Ghetto

How do you teach these children? What do they need from you?

Children from the ghetto need an understanding of their problems, structure, and positiveness (high expectations plus optimism).

Need for Understanding

You have walked many mornings through the community, visited homes (sometimes with a community worker), and spoken to community people. You begin to see that the children's background and their attitudes of despair, defeat, and expectation are products of it. The teacher who shuts her mind to the world of the child has shut off an integral part of him and it cripples her means of coping with his problems.

Realistically, children of the ghetto color your teaching day with certain behavior which often defeats the new teacher and discourages the more experienced one. You will meet:

Defiance of Authority: These children are quite adept at finding the teacher's Achilles heel. They are often rebellious in class and uninhibited in behavior, testing limits and patience, and ascertaining the direction the teacher will take. "Sit down John!" you shout authoritatively. "You make me teacher!" he answers adamantly. You subsequently find through bitter experience that a half hour of hassling plus the intervention of the supervisor will coax him into his seat. Somehow both of you have lost. The next time you try a softer approach, "Please sit down John." He looks puzzled for a moment and then responds without comment. You have given him the respect as an individual that he wants without demeaning either yourself or him. The same approach does not work with all children. Nothing seems to work with some. There are children who must not be met head-on with an authoritarian approach; John is one. It will take skill, perception, and sensitivity to deal with some of these emotionally inflammable youngsters in a soothing manner.

Academic Failure: Failure in the ghetto is no stranger. Children repeat grades with surprising frequency. Many families have at least one member who has been held over at least once in the elementary school. It has become accepted. Usually the third grade is the crucial one, and by this time the retaining has already taken place.

The criterion for this is usually a reading retardation level of two years. Retardation in math is usually a close runner-up. If you are fortunate to have the top class on the grade, most of your children would probably be reading on grade level, whereas in a middle-class school this would be an average class. The norm, then, is depressed in terms of reading scores. Yours will be the task of elevating these poor reading scores and fostering an enthusiasm for reading which may preferably be done with an individualized reading approach.

Lack of Motivation from Home: There seems to be some division of opinion on this issue. It might seem to you that the child's home lacks motivation, yet Sears and Maccoby in their work, *Patterns of Child Rearing,* found that deprived parents have a greater degree of interest that their children succeed in elementary school than do middle-class parents.[1] Yet the lower class is more pragmatic about college. The fact is that "The average deprived person is interested in education in terms of how useful and practical it can be to him. Education provides the means for more and different kinds of employment, provides a more secure future. Jobs that interest him like fireman, policeman, postal clerk, all require fairly detailed civil service examinations,

---

[1] Robert R. Sears, Eleanor E. Maccoby, and Harry Levin, *Patterns of Child Rearing* (Evanston, Ill.: Row, Peterson & Company, 1957), p. 430.

and education is sorely needed to obtain these coveted positions."[2]

What you will find in your meetings with ghetto parents is that there is less reading matter in the home for the child to be exposed to, fewer books and magazines. You must meet this challenge in school through providing the child with library facilities in and out of the school, and giving him individualized reading tailored to his needs and interests.

Obscenity: You may meet an uninhibited barrage of obscenities and you should avoid evidence of being shocked or being personally insulted. Many of these expressions are used without too much forethought, and with little restraint. The momma insult is usually not tied in with anyone's momma in particular, but represents a kind of badge of honor for parties involved. As is frequently the case, the one doing the momma cursing has the most mixed-up relationship with his own mother. Sloughing it off in many instances will calm down the agitation.

Reasoning during a heated exchange just doesn't work here. For example, you try to intercept an accelerating ranking-out session with a plea, "Why do you curse his mother when you don't even know her?" He retorts graphically, "What do you mean I don't know his mother? She's sittin on a garbage truck right now," and the exchange is intensified. You find you must accept a good portion of the talk, perhaps with humor, skillfully learning to divert it into other channels.

If the use of obscenities becomes excessive in the classroom, then group discussion should be held on the reasons for the use of improper language. In these discussions children will make an assessment and commitment to find some other means of self-expression. However, lectures denouncing obscenities, in which children do not participate, will fall on deaf ears. The best control for inappropriate language in the classroom is constructive class activities such as clay modeling, providing outlets for the children in which aggressiveness and repressed hostilities can find release.

---

[2] Frank Riessman, *The Culturally Deprived Child* (New York: Harper & Row, Publishers, 1962), p.13.

Lack of Respect: An informal survey of the problems beginning teachers encountered was conducted in one ghetto school.

The results ranked lack of respect toward the teachers at the top of a list of twenty items.

The young teacher enters the classroom expecting to be venerated for her new license and position. Instead she falls victim to inattentive children, is frequently talked back to, and is sometimes jeered at. She struggles for identity and some dignity as a teacher. A position of respect with the children is one that has to be earned. This is true not only in the ghetto but also in middle-class schools. She has a trial by fire and must prove her mettle. The additional hurdle in the ghetto is a subtle one. Implicit in the children's respect for her is her own respect for the children as individuals. There are children who cannot read, have difficulty in following directions, are neglected, frequently dirty, rebellious, unresponsive to conventional discipline, and at times seem like alien creatures; these children must be respected for the individuals they are and be helped to develop if the teacher is to earn their respect.

Structure

Many ghetto children have two things in common, uncertainty and lack of routine. A father is present one day and disappears the next. Homes are disordered, broken up by desertion, some wracked by violence and many suffering with economic deprivation. There are children who rely for their breakfasts on special programs set up in the schools. They are never certain what the next moment brings.

You can supply this need for structure in your classroom. Structure can be set up by:

- Maintaining a few simple rules which should be understood by the children and even partly formulated by them.
- Consistency in carrying through these rules.

Have a few (e.g., three) rules at the start and carry them out. The new teacher commits the error of composing a battery of rules and regulations which she imposes upon a group which would struggle to maintain only one. You can then expand when you have achieved success. Remember that the goal is consistency and not numbers.

Structure and Creativity: Does the creative teacher who allows freedom of movement and thought need this structure? And what about those teachers involved in new programs such as the open classroom?

Even in the most permissive open classroom, structure is built in by thorough preplanning by the teacher of activities and tasks to be undertaken by the children. Children in their creative explorings must have a sense of order. To create anything in the classroom there must be structure and limits set or there will be chaos. One classroom in which the children appeared to have full reign, and which a permissive teacher described as creative chaos, was in actuality a class with definite limits. The fact was that the children knew exactly how far to go before they began their activity. Together they had planned simple rules which each child understood. When one child exceeded the limits, a reproval from the teacher sent him back to his seat.

Positiveness vs. Defeat

In the small group of teachers that met in my office in Chapter Three ("The Teacher Works with the Counselor"), we came to the realization through our discussions of the ghetto child that our own attitudes toward our work definitely affected the child. *Tension on the part of the teacher breeds restless children and the children are doomed with the teacher's defeated outlook.*

Having dealt with the ghetto child in both the classroom and counselor's office for many years, I can make an emphatic statement that the ghetto child has an enormous untapped potential, and is a reservoir for creative talent. But it is lost in the handicap of poor academic ability. It is often in his self-expression through art and the dramatic form that originality and creativity have a chance to shine through.

However, ghetto children may not be as nonverbal as they are generally thought to be. Irving Taylor, formerly Project Coordinator of the Staff of the Institute for Developmental Studies, "finds on word association tests that deprived children give responses that are often less conventional, more unusual, original, and independent. They seem to be more flexible and visual with language. For example, to the word 'stone,' deprived children are more willing to give associations such as 'solid' and 'hard'; responses that encompass the perceptual qualities of the object."[3]

One kindergarten child in my ghetto school returning from a nature trip said aloud to the teacher, "This bark is the clothes of the tree." She was holding bits of this clothing in her hand. What five-year-old response from any social milieu can match this imagery?

Like every child in the world, the children of the ghetto react to praise and general approval. But the ghetto child has been steeped in failure. He must be given encouragement constantly. (Yet all children thrive on encouragement. So do adults.) The schools must provide experiences for successful living. Where there are problems, we can offer to help the parent cope with his or hers through professional assistance, but it is the child to whom we are committed. If we approach the problems of teaching him with encouragement and high expectations, he can succeed.

Looking at the Ghetto Teacher

Who is the ghetto teacher? She is frequently new, usually young, white, and female. After a few years of an uphill fight she may resign, her leaving frequently lost in the shuffle of other teacher turnovers. If she remains, she gains experience and competence, and after five years becomes a paragon of teaching skills to the less experienced. Brief sketches are given here of three teachers, each at different stages of her career.

Miss Goodwin Doesn't Understand: The New Teacher

Miss Goodwin is new to the classroom and she doesn't understand that she has all the abilities for succeeding with these children. She is talented but lacks the self-confidence to proceed and develop her own potential. She looks with reverance at her colleague, Mrs. Kessler, a stern-looking individual who succeeds with one grimace in silencing her class, whose voice sends a clap of thunder into the classroom. Miss Goodwin imitates this and the

---

[3] Frank Riessman, *The Culturally Deprived Child* (New York: Harper & Row, Publishers, 1962), p.77.

children laugh. "Your face looks funny teacher, when you look mad" one small voice says, and she is crestfallen.

Miss Goodwin then looks desperately for a magic formula, thinking of her own inadequacies. So she attempts a painting lesson she has seen in Miss Coleman's room. Ignorant of the planning which has preceded it, she panics when Richard paints Picasso-like designs on Jill's face. Miss Goodwin doesn't understand that she has a corresponding ability in music and could successfully put together a rhythm band and a glee club.

What Miss Goodwin doesn't realize is that although she can learn from the experienced, she must develop her own strengths. This is especially essential in the ghetto, where new approaches utilizing individual teacher talents are the bulwarks of creative and effective teaching. Good routines and sensitive supervision are requisites, but ultimately she and her children must come to acknowledge all the capabilities that are uniquely hers.

Most colleges turn out teachers in one mold; it is the children, then, who single them out in their innate sensitivity and highlight their differences. The youngsters do this swiftly and accurately and the teachers stagger, searching for who they really are as educators. The activity which Miss Goodwin will have the most success with will be the one which comes from her basic interests; the knowledge and enthusiasm for it will be contagious; the children will catch it.

Miss Goodwin doesn't understand this yet, but she will be guided by a perceptive supervisor who will encourage her to develop her own uniqueness. She will find in time that she has a talent for committee work and can plunge into a class unit with ease. She will find that she has the ability to work on an individualized reading program, departing from the traditional group approach; she will enjoy watching the progress of each child as he selects reading matter keyed to his interests and abilities. She is developing as a teacher, leaving behind an unsure girl who entered the classroom groping for ways to prove herself. Ultimately, in the natural scheme of things, another new teacher will look into her classroom, hoping to glean techniques and painfully attempt to emulate that which is uniquely Miss Goodwin. It is a cycle which is unending.

About Miss Thomas: The Experienced Teacher

Miss Thomas is not a new teacher, nor is she struggling to establish herself. She is an effective teacher in the ghetto; she also happens to be black. One wonders what powers intervened for her to achieve this success. In an interview with Miss Thomas I had planned to learn all about her special "tips" for teachers, but what resulted was not entirely the case.

Miss Thomas projected an air of authority to her colleagues, yet what she revealed was that beneath this was a share of misgivings and doubts. "All teachers have them to some degree. There are times that I feel that I am not a good enough teacher, that I am not achieving what I should. When I started, these feelings were most intense. The stuff-the-information-into-their-little-minds routine was paramount, but after awhile, I learned to relax and pace myself and children didn't run away."

"But," I asked, "how can you still have doubts after so many years? You're regarded as being quite expert."

"Well I do, and contrary to the perfection that some teachers would have you believe they possess, the really concerned teacher is always evaluating herself, seeking new ways because circumstances change. Don't get me wrong. I know that basically I'm an effective teacher, but there are times that I question what I'm doing."

"Do you think that being black helps with these children?"

"It helps in part," Miss Thomas answered. "Black children may have identification with a black teacher. However, the ingredients for good teaching have nothing to do with color. Children respond to the teacher's personality and competency, and I might add, humanity. A teacher, if anything, must be humane and tuned in to the children's needs, providing a meaningful curriculum."

"How do you have such marvelous results with your classes?"

"My standards are high for myself and for the class. I always feel that they can do better than they have in the past, and there is an anxiety to succeed. I believe the anxiety has to be there."

"What about motivation?"

"These children can be motivated to learn but you must start where the child is and make the activities mean something. Isn't relevancy the word that is generally used? The parents of these children are frequently blamed, but if you've spoken to enough parents you find out quickly that they want them to do well. The trouble is that in many instances their parents cannot provide them with the attention and additional tutoring the children need."

"Do you think that teacher expectation plays a part?"

"Most definitely! One needs to cut through years of apathy and failure with these kids, and even I sometimes don't succeed," she laughed. "What really amazes these children is when they see you really care about them and what they do, then they produce."

"And you expect your slowest classes to produce?"

"I guess I'm an oddball for thinking it, but some of my most creative children come from these classes. They are unusual in a nonacademic way. Remember the play we put on last year?" Miss Thomas remained undaunted and smilingly concluded this interview.

What the author gleaned from this meeting were not routines of discipline and work habits, but rather an attitude of optimism and openness, of constant self-appraisal and flexibility, and a kind of stubborn refusal to capitulate to the general expectation of defeat. Miss Thomas is a truly creative teacher, although assessing creativity was not the purpose of this interview. She is always creating a new optimistic design for classroom living. And this optimism is tempered by the harshest master of them all, her own self-criticism. All good teachers have this dynamism in common, for it is what makes them adapt to each new wave of youngsters. The reason that Miss Thomas strives for higher goals for the youngsters is simple. She knows that the children can make it.

About Mrs. Caldera: The Teacher Leaving

And what about the teacher who is leaving the school? How does she feel about the time she has invested in teaching children? Perhaps, as in this hypothetical letter, it is with mixed feelings that she leaves. And as in this letter it is with an optimistic note for the future.

Dear Children,

As you know, I've left the school to have a baby. Of course you must know my feelings because I have been with many of you for two years as I went from the fifth to the sixth grade.

It's difficult for me to put down on paper some of the things I feel. I was both happy and sad when I left. I was depressed because I looked at the neighborhood where I taught these past six years and saw the same ugly buildings standing and your problems growing more serious. But then, I thought of some of the things we had done together and I decided to write down some of my thoughts and feelings.

If you remember, at the start of the year it was so hard to make progress with you Patricia and you James. It seemed as though you were fighting me and nothing I did made any difference. The turning point came when the boys said they were sorry for causing so much trouble. We then did the Social Studies Unit on China and planned our class mural.

I hope Patricia that the trouble we spoke of is gone and James, you have stopped your fighting. I feel sad about what you said James, that you expected me to leave because everybody goes away from you. You must realize by now that I am not purposely leaving the class.

I wonder what each of you is thinking now as you go on to junior high school. Will you sometimes remember some of the funny things that happened in our class like Richard always clowning, and the time he put two legs in one pants leg of his costume and laughed so hard that he fell off the chair? Will you remember the good things like painting the mural, the trip to the United Nations, our play about drugs and the poetry we wrote?

Some of you spoke in social studies of how you hated the neighborhood you lived in and the fact that it is a slum. Perhaps when you grow older, you can do something to change all that by being the kind of people you really want to be. Maybe something of what we spoke about and did in class really counted. Will you think about it?

Affectionately yours,
Lisa Caldera
(your teacher)

Creativity in the Ghetto

Where are the children in the ghetto who are creatively talented but are grossly retarded in academic skills? We cannot rely upon a parent for coaching, assistance from a mother who is fighting for her family's economic survival. These children with creative promise and sitting in slow classes exist in full measure; they are children such as Dwight.

Dwight is now an adult. He, for all purposes, has fallen into obscurity. But it need not have been that way. Dwight, however, like his many brothers in the ghetto, had poor reading skills and was lost in the shuffle of a huge welfare family.

He was nine years of age when my class put on a performance of Peter Pan. The class was the slowest fourth year on the grade. I was considered foolish by my colleagues for attempting an original play using the theme of Peter Pan with a class of this sort. But rashness and youth make excellent bedfellows and I ventured on. We began to improvise roles, delineating the one of Peter Pan. We tried different children in various roles and then it happened.

Dwight stepped forward. He stood with his torn shirt, ripped trousers and *became* Peter Pan, and sang the Mary Martin excerpts which I threw at him with disbelief. He jumped about our makeshift stage like a professional, and I knew that moment that it was not just the fulfillment of a role. Dwight had an enormous creative talent. The expectations of the next few weeks raised myself and the class to near delirium. We improvised a pirate's dance on the heels of this dramatic find, disregarding all the rules of choreography and whipped on by a fever of approaching success. A sewing committee of three girls made the costumes and we covered Dwight with a green crepe paper tunic as in Figure 12-1. His handsome black face glowed.

As a result of an amazing performance by Dwight in the assembly, the school counselor obtained a dramatic scholarship for him. But his success was short-lived. Two months later, Dwight moved down South to stay with his grandmother. The separation of hundreds of miles and the break-up of a family erased our ties.

Dwight undoubtedly was a phenomenon. It had taken four years of sitting in academically slow classes for his talent to emerge, and a few months to lose it.

FIGURE 12-1

When talent and creativity are suppressed, it has been found that this repression can cause psychological disturbances, and in the ghetto this creativity when not uncovered can give way to delinquent behavior.

Torrence has stated that "the expression of creative desires brings upon the individual certain sanctions which produce tensions. Without the proper guidance, he finds it necessary to distort or abandon his creativity in one or more ways." [4] Added to this, the creative ghetto child who is slow academically and poor in skills is doubly fettered by his limitations. Like Dwight, he may be put into a class for the dull and left to smolder. This smoldering may eventually develop into disruptive behavior and extinguish whatever facets of creative talent may have been developing. It is the function of the school, then, to find and nurture creative talent and help reduce the handicap of poor academic skills. This is not solely for the child's natural develop-

---

[4] Adapted from E. Paul Torrance, *Guiding Creative Talent* (Englewood Cliffs, N.J.: Prentice Hall, 1962), p.133.

ment but also as a bulwark against the potentially destructive energy in a thwarted youngster.

Mental Health Services in the Ghetto

There is a distorted kind of logic which places the same number of guidance counselors in the ghetto schools as in the middle-class schools. Children needing therapy in middle-class and more affluent areas may be referred to private psychiatrists, while the ghetto child desperately depends upon school and free clinical services.

The staggering problem of inadequate mental health facilities in the ghetto is so intolerable that I was prompted to write "A Future for Jennifer," showing that in the face of this dearth of facilities, there was little any of us could do.

Jennifer was a child born into violence. Her father was given to drunken rages. Jennifer grew up in a kind of daze. The marital strife affected her, finally spilling over into her school behavior. Jennifer was sent to a state mental health hospital, then released but not cured; she was sent back again into the very confused environment that nurtured her illness.

"If Jennifer was Alice in Wonderland in a dreamlike world, we were the Mad Hatters in not giving her the help she needed, residential placement in a structured situation, a living situation with proper psychiatric treatment. There is a limited number of such places open, particularly for black Protestant children. Our black children with deep emotional problems are finally sent to state training schools as a resolution for antisocial behavior. They never learn to live with others in our society."[5]

There was a tragic lack of adequate mental health services. What happened here? One counselor tried to help Jennifer; one psychologist, overloaded with cases, saw her briefly; a state hospital dealt with her in a cursory fashion, returning her prematurely to the school; the courts couldn't meet her problems. There was inadequate family counseling for the parents. There is a need, then, for all disciplines working with these children to be intensified. There must be a reduction of the teacher-pupil ratio

---

[5]"A Future for Jennifer," Changing Education Supplement, *American Teacher*, (Washington, D.C.: American Federation of Teachers) 56, No. 6, Feb. 1972, pp. 15,20.

and the counselor-pupil ratio in these areas, and the doubling and tripling of existing guidance services in the schools. There must be a corresponding increase in school psychologists and consulting psychiatrists.

It is not for the child alone that these services must exist in the ghetto but also for the teacher; the counselor's role has to be one of close relationship to the problems of the classroom, in planning curricula suitable to the special needs of these children and in devising innovative programs developing the children's abilities. The ghettos are sending out distress signals for their children, but few are listening.

New Approaches Needed

Teacher Preparation

A college coordinator for student teachers asked what could be suggested to acquaint her students with the kinds of problems they would most likely meet in the ghetto.

Prior preparation of these teachers for working with the ghetto child, an area to which these new teachers would most likely be assigned, is sorely needed as part of the college program.

One way of determining the needs of teacher preparation is to interview the ghetto teacher herself. In answer to the question, "How can you be prepared for working in this area?" the following responses resulted:

It won't make any difference. Experience is the best teacher.

I think the teacher should have a transition period after student teaching in which she has control of the class at least three times a week with someone advising her.

The trouble with student teaching is that the situation is unreal! There's always someone advising you and protecting you.

The course preparation for teaching is all wrong. You have too much theory and only one year of student teaching. You should have at least two years of on-the-job learning in a kind of work-study period.

The college teachers should come down and see what these children are doing. They would then revise their courses. Every few years they should be required to come into the ghetto or any elementary school and work with the teachers and see their problems.

In college you have ideal situations. You really don't have to face any problems. The preparation is all wrong and has nothing to do with these kids.

Did you ask me what I need? Forget it. It's the first week of the year and I need a vacation.

It was interesting that the general feeling of the teachers was that the professors who are giving these courses are not acquainted with some of the problems of the ghetto. The teachers wanted a closer relationship between the college instructor, his student, and the school into which his student is assigned. They felt that there is often a cleavage between the middle-class standards of the college courses and the hard facts that the teacher must meet with in the ghetto classroom. Colleges have now begun to change their teaching programs by increasing the student teaching experience in the elementary schools.

Need for Male Image

There is a need in the ghetto for more male teachers, and counselors as well as male supervisors. It is on this early level where the need for a male image is vital to a child lacking one in his home. In this way the boy can have someone he can emulate and who can supply him with a living model of the manner in which a man should behave. Except for administrators, the elementary school is in many cases essentially a female teacher's domain in contrast with junior and senior high schools. Encouragement of more male school personnel to enter the elementary school level would help fulfill this need.

Individually Guided Non-Graded Instruction

The holdover rate in the ghetto area is appalling. There are children sitting in classrooms for an additional year who are fairly good in math but are very slow in reading. They sit with colleagues one year younger than themselves; there is reinforcement of further feelings of shame and failure and they are bored, bored, bored because they are repeating what they feel is "baby work." Often the child's reading improves little because now he is aware of his disgrace, and it adds an additional emotional block to an already damaged learning capacity, rather than being an incentive for increased efforts. The holdover system is psychologically damaging, and does little academically. Few efforts have been made to actually evaluate the reading results at the end of the repeated year.

The child, possibly with creative potential, is made to repeat a grade, hoping that he will catch up. In the ghetto, this just doesn't happen. All that has been accomplished is that the failure reinforcement is beginning to operate.

One alternative to this is individually guided education. Here the school makes a break with the century-old practice of graded education. In March, 1971, the U.S. Office of Education selected the multiunit elementary school for nationwide installation and provided funding to initiate and coordinate the effort. For example, the Wisconsin Readskill Skill Development is organized into six skill areas; word attack, study skills, comprehension, self-directed reading, interpretive skills, and creative skills.[6]

"The Multiunit Elementary School (MES) is the support vehicle for achieving IGE. Non-graded instructional units replace age-graded classes...

Typically, each child is involved each day in one-to-one relations with a teacher or aide, independent study, and small-group, class-size and large-group activities. The proportional amount of each activity is based on each particular child's characteristics, the objectives to be attained, the nature of available instructional materials, and the cost of instruction."[7]

Bilingual Teaching Programs

In many schools there is an influx of children from various countries. Bilingual programs have been established to meet the

---

[6] Adapted from *Individually Guided Education and the Multiunit Elementary School*, Wisconsin Research and Development Center for Cognitive Learning, the University of Wisconsin, Madison, Wisconsin, Seventh Annual Report, 1970-1971, pp. 2-10.

[7] *Staff Development Bulletin No. 5*, Division of Recruitment, Training and Staff Development, Office of Personnel, Board of Education of the City of New York, Brooklyn, New York, January, 1972, p. 4.

needs of special classroom instruction for children who are learning English as a second language. In some schools there is only one bilingual class per grade when there may be a need for more. The lack of these special classes necessitates the newly arrived bilingual child to be placed in regular classes; he is left struggling with the difficulty of learning a new language in a strange culture. In the case of the bilingual child living in the ghetto there are the additional problems of ghetto life. Frequently these children are neglected in school and become traumatized and withdrawn. Many Spanish children, for example, are frequently thought of as retarded because of their failure to respond in class. There remains a great need for additional instructional programs for bilingual children in all schools that these children attend.

Tutorial Programs

Other approaches, such as the tutorial programs of working with individual children as in Chapter Eight, apply very aptly to the ghetto child.

Problem-Solving

There should be an increase in creative problem-solving classroom methods. This was illustrated in Chapter Ten, where class meetings were originally used with disadvantaged children and proven effective. Such meetings provide children with a verbal release.

Role-Playing

Children in the ghetto should be exposed to more sociodrama. Role-playing is a natural outlet for the disadvantaged child because it overcomes his verbal limitations and provides for exploration of solutions to social problems.

Supportive Teacher Discussion Groups

More supportive teacher discussion workshops are needed so that the teacher can release her tensions and explore her feelings and attitudes toward daily problems of coping and reduce feelings of alienation. Generally, teacher-counselor workshops are held on a voluntary basis and in many instances the teacher who is in the most need of morale boosting does not attend.

Developing Teacher Talents

Further development of the skills of the teacher is needed. The teachers have talents which are frequently being overlooked. One teacher had a talent for choreography which was confined to her classroom and at that, infrequently used. Another had a talent for art, which should have been used on a school-wide basis. A school curriculum, traditionally oriented, frequently has no place for these interests. In order to reach the children's interests, we are going to have to deal with the teachers on a more personal level, developing their full potential as individuals, and utilizing all their abilities. The fact remains that in the last analysis, it is going to be the creative teacher who will truly reach the ghetto child, because it is this teacher who will be open to new avenues of approach.

Individualization and Smaller Classes

There is a need for more specially funded individualized instruction for ghetto youngsters in terms of improving reading skills. But in order to accomplish this individualization there must be smaller class size so that a closer relationship between the child and teacher can be achieved.

Class size is a crucial factor in classrooms. One cannot effectively teach in classrooms of over 25 youngsters in which a third may be guidance problems. Certainly the establishment of any special programs involving individualization will be ineffective with a large group.

Summary

Teachers deal with the special problems of the ghetto youngster with an approach stressing attitudes of understanding, need for structure, and higher expectations. Sketches of three teachers are given, one new, one an effective experienced teacher, and one leaving the system. They point up the necessity of developing teacher individuality, meeting the children's needs optimistically, resourcefully, and with empathy.

Creativity exists in the ghetto but is hampered by academic limitations. The creatively gifted child frequently sits in the slowest class on the grade and is consistently thwarted. This creativity, if suppressed, can lead to aberrant behavior.

There is a shortage of mental health facilities in the ghetto. The need for additional counselors and psychologists in the schools is urgent, as are adequate diagnostic and treatment facilities and family counseling services.

New approaches for dealing with the ghetto youngster include improved teacher education, the non-graded concept eliminating the holdover system, bilingual programs, more teacher discussion groups, more role-playing and use of peer groups as in tutoring, smaller class size and individualized instruction.

Chapter Thirteen

"I see the mind of a five-year-old as a volcano with two vents; destructiveness and creativeness. And I see that to the extent that we widen the creative channel, we atrophy the destructive one."[1]

Guidance Through Creativity

"Creativity" is a means through which the child can be reached, but the word is misunderstood. "Be creative," the overworked slogan of the teaching profession, is confusing and possibly disturbing to the new teacher. She confuses creativity and talent; she sees herself as either talented or not (usually in the arts) and hence she is either creative or not. But she really need not be talented to be creative, because creativity is largely an attitude. The creative person lives life more intensely than most, feels things a bit more deeply, and uses unorthodox means a bit more freely. He is perhaps more extreme, yet paradoxically more sensible than others.

The Meaning of Creativity

Creativity has been described by many. It is basically the creation of something new and fresh from existing forms. Alice Miel states, "It appears to be a deliberate process of making a new combination or patterning of materials, movements, words, symbols or ideas and somehow making the product available to others, visibly or otherwise."[2]

The creative teacher must be unafraid to explore the unknown with the children; unafraid to take a hackneyed curriculum, use elements of it and devise new plans and activities

---

[1] Sylvia Ashton-Warner, *Teacher* (New York: Bantam Books, Inc., 1964), p.29.

[2] Alice Miel, *Creativity in Teaching* (Belmont, California: Wadsworth Publishing Company, Inc., 1961), p.6.

to meet the needs of the children. It may involve improvising and much trial and error, but in this exploration new, more relevant planning may evolve tailored to the children's daily needs. No amount of prescribed curriculum, no planned course can reach the untapped potential of a blocked youngster like a creative teacher.

To reach children who are unreachable may take listening to the beat of "a different drummer" in the words of Thoreau. To be creative is to be courageous, but it is more! It is a way of thinking and perceiving new relationships. Creativity may be dormant in teachers and needs to be awakened, or it may be vital and functioning. Guidance through creativity is an approach for helping the disruptive as well as the average, the slow as well as the gifted child.

Creative Teaching: An Approach to the Disruptive

The creative approach to teaching presents the same material in new ways. Let's see how it works! A class studying social studies is bored. As a result they became noisy and disruptive. The class was difficult, slow in reading, with several disruptive children and many with short attention spans. Mrs. Kahn appraised the situation and saw that the lesson could not continue. She had planned to present this lesson for observation by her supervisor. Children were to study Peter Zenger, the issue of freedom of the press and present short written reports. The children frankly were not interested. Freedom of the press had little meaning in their lives and they couldn't care less about poor Mr. Zenger and his old newspaper, which was out of print anyway.

The class was sophisticated in the media of television, and often members came to school with eyes heavy-lidded from late night viewing. They knew the intricacies of the medical and legal professions, being aware of such terms as "ventricular fibulation" and "corpus delicti" from the various programs. Mrs. Kahn capitalized on this background. She chose one of these glorious professions, Law. She discarded the conventional compositions and launched the entire class into the jury trial of Peter Zenger in the true spirit of Perry Mason.

A brief warm-up period consisting of discussion and procedure was required. Children volunteered for the roles of commentator, counsel for the defense, prosecutor, judge, Peter Zenger,

202   Guidance Through Creativity

jurors, bailiff and court clerk, and the remainder were spectators.

When Mr. Miller entered the classroom, he was amazed to be escorted by a bailiff of the court to the back seat provided for him in the courtroom.

The trial had begun. It was an Educational Television Production with John, the Commentator, introducing the production. "This is Walter Crankase presenting the exciting Peter Zenger Trial. Watch closely folks and see who wins!"

Peter Zenger was eloquently defended by his attorney, William (a very volatile class problem), who got carried away in his enthusiasm and almost let James, the prosecutor, "have it right in the nose." The Judge, Nancy, a female anachronism, did an effective job with her gavel, threatening to clear the court at the slightest infraction. But James precipitated an historical innacuracy in one of the improvisations by winning the case. In fact, historical inaccuracies ran rampant throughout all four productions, but no one really minded. They put on the trial before other classes on the grade due to the request of Mr. Miller.

The children's understanding of the issues and their enthusiasm more than compensated for any errors in the improvisations.

Boredom can be a villain in the classroom, for it is the death knell of the creative promise of children. Children must be continually stimulated by new ways of presenting old material. Creative teaching also seizes on those stimuli which arise from the children themselves, and creates anew. For example, take the case of Suzie and her cat, Julius.

Class 5-5 and a Creative Teacher's Influence

Class 5-5 was a special group; they were very bright, far ahead academically, and had several very talented children. Suzie was one. Their teacher, Mrs. Teller, was sensitive to the children's needs and open to new experiences that could be used as a springboard for classroom activities. This year Class 5-5 was to write a story about a cat named Sir Julius and use the multi-media approach of writing, art, dramatics, tape recording, and film-making using transparencies. And they could do it because Mrs. Teller, their teacher, saw herself as reacting to the children's needs in a creative and involved way. It happened this way:

Suzie, a quiet, sensitive child, had a cat named Julius. One day she appeared in school apparently troubled. When Mrs. Teller spoke to her, Suzie tearfully recounted the experiences of her cat.

"My neighbor says my cat is arrogant. What does that mean, Mrs. Teller?"

"It's something like haughty or stuck-up," the teacher answered. "But Suzie, all cats are a bit arrogant and haughty."

Mrs. Teller thought for a moment. "Would you like to write a story about it? You could work together with the four girls on the writing committee and that mean neighbor of yours could be one of the characters. How does that appeal to you?"

Suzie's eyes lit up and she added, "I could call it 'Julius, the arrogant cat'." She smiled and brushed her tears.

The writing committee was enthusiastic about the idea when it was broached. They obtained their information from Suzie about Julius's problem of being arrogant and their imaginations took over from there. Doris thought of the character of the cat doctor, Dr. Tweedle, because her own cat was taken to a veterinarian and Lisa thought of the ending for Sir Julius. Mrs.

FIGURE 13-1

Teller was very enthusiastic and advised the girls about the dialogue of such characters as Mrs. Quiggly and Dr. Tweedle. She showed that the use of repetitive statements, such as "How true, how true, how true," in the case of Dr. Tweedle could make him appear bizarre. They also discussed the use of figures of speech, such as "chip on the shoulder." All this was compiled by Amy, Doris, and Lisa, but the final writing was executed by Suzie, a child with considerable writing ability, under the guidance of Mrs. Teller. To further motivate the character development, Mrs. Teller drew the picture, shown in Figure 13-1, of Dr. Tweedle and Sir Julius.

In the words of Suzie, "The purpose of the tale is to show that because a person (or cat) may appear disagreeable, he may really be quite lonely and you should try to understand that. Appearances are not always as they seem." After the story was read to the class, a boy jumped up and said, "Why Julius is just like me — maybe that's why people don't like me!"

As Suzie stood in front of another fifth-year class, she told the following story of Julius:

Sir Julius, the Arrogant Cat

Sir Julius was sitting on Mrs. Quiggly's porch making her very nervous.

"Your cat is arrogant and there is simply no doubt about it!" Mrs. Quiggly said to Suzie.

"Arrogant?" Suzie echoed.

"Yes, arrogant! I have watched him for some time now, slink up to my porch and sit there as though he owned it, and just stare at me with that funny look. He makes me nervous. When I tell him to go away, he doesn't budge. He's arrogant and that's all there is about it. You ought to do something about him. He has no business being that way."

"Does arrogant mean being stuck-up?" Suzie asked. She felt very bad about her cat being the word Mrs. Quiggly said.

"Arrogant is worse than stuck-up. Arrogant is arrogant, and that's that!" Mrs. Quiggly shouted.

Suzie tried again. "Is arrogant the same as rude and impolite?"

Mrs. Quiggly shouted louder, "Arrogant is worse than rude and impolite. Arrogant is one of the most terrible things a cat can be. I have spoken to your mother many times about Sir Julius and his attitude. Such an attitude should be corrected in a cat."

"I'll see if I can do something about it," said Suzie.

"I really wish you would because he gives me a nervous feeling in my stomach if I see him on the porch."

Suzie called, "Here Julius, come." Sir Julius gave Mrs. Quiggly his haughty arrogant stare, hunched his back, stiffened his tail and walked past her.

"Oh my heavens," Mrs. Quiggly exclaimed. "There he goes again. I just can't look at him."

"I'm very sorry Mrs. Quiggly. I'll see to it that it doesn't happen again."

Suzie walked down the street with Sir Julius trailing behind her.

Suzie thought about when she first found Sir Julius when he was only a baby kitten. Julius as a baby was very friendly with not a trace of haughtiness about him. She had named him Julius after a favorite uncle of hers. He was a pretty kitten, light grey with white mittens on his paws. At least his fur looked like white mittens. They all lived in a bad neighborhood which her father had called a "slum." She remembered that there were broken bottles in the street and houses with windows missing from them. Sometimes people would be fighting in the street. But there were plenty of cats for Julius to play with. He was happy. Then Suzie's mother and father moved with Julius to a lovely old house which had a garden in which Julius could play. There Julius grew up into a cat. Perhaps the neighbors were unkind to Julius because he became quieter, a little shy and walked around with what Suzie's father called a "chip on his shoulder." Suzie did not see anything on Julius's shoulder but she supposed that it was something only adults saw. Then she decided that the name Julius was not dignified enough. She decided to knight him "Sir Julius." She took a toy sword and put it over Julius's shoulder, the one with the invisible chip on it, and proclaimed in a very loud voice, "I knight thee, 'Sir Julius.' After that Sir Julius became very dignified and very arrogant. He was as arrogant as Mrs. Quiggly said.

Suzie was not sure what "arrogant" meant. When she took Julius home after her visit with Mrs. Quiggly, she looked up the word a-r-r-o-g-a-n-t in the dictionary. The dictionary said, "disposed to make great claim of rank or importance." She knew now that arrogant was difinitely something like being stuck up. "I guess that he's really arrogant. But what is there to do about it?" She thought that perhaps a doctor could cure him and make him more friendly. She didn't want him going through life with everyone hating him.

Suzie coaxed her mother and father into taking Sir Julius to a cat doctor, a veterinarian, Dr. Tweedle.

Dr. Tweedle was a fat jolly cat doctor with whiskers under his nose and glasses at the tip of his nose. He kept shaking and nodding his head and muttering, "How true, how true, how true." He looked closely at Sir Julius and asked him questions in a kind of cat language that only Dr. Tweedle understood.

"Yes, yes, yes, yes" he muttered. "How true, how true, how true. This is a very serious problem brought about by the fact that he misses his old cat friends. The cats on your block are not very friendly to him, neither are the grownups, I might add. I will give him some pink pills to sweeten his stomach and disposition. Suzie, give these to him three times a day with his catnip and come back in a month's time to see if there is any difference. Yes, yes, yes, yes. How true, how true, how true. A very sad case," he said, shaking his head and pulling his whiskers. At this moment his whiskers looked very much like Sir Julius's.

Suzie wiped a tear out of her eye and gathered poor Sir Julius up in her arms. She suddenly said, "Oh! Dr. Tweedle, I almost forgot. My father said he has a chip on his shoulder although I really can't see it."

"Hm---mm," said Dr. Tweedle. "It isn't too bad. The pills will be good for that too." Suzie was a bit happier now. She took the box of pink pills and locked them up in a special place in her desk. Faithfully, she fed them to Sir Julius three times a day with catnip. She added a bit of milk to make sure that he didn't get heartburn like Aunt Sarah always had from her pills.

A week later Suzie met Mrs. Quiggly on the street. She fearfully asked, "Do you — eh — see any difference in Sir Julius, Mrs. Quiggly — I hope?"

"He seems the same to me," yelled Mrs. Quiggly. "Maybe a bit nastier. He's getting a bit older though. He won't live forever, you know."

Suzie felt like saying, "You nasty old woman" but didn't because Suzie was well brought up. Suzie kept feeding Sir Julius the pink pills along with his catnip until the pills were all gone. She had to admit that Sir Julius looked exactly the same. He was a stuck-up, haughty and arrogant cat and had not changed one drop.

She took him back to Dr. Tweedle. Dr. Tweedle shook his head, "Yes, yes, yes, yes. How true, how true, how true. He has indeed a problem. He has no friends, that's his trouble. Take him back to his own neighborhood and let him stay with his friends for a while."

Suzie and her father drove Sir Julius back but it was all different. Sir Julius had left as a kitten and was now a cat. No cats recognized him. Some cats had even moved away to better neighborhoods. He sniffed about and made a face. "After all, it was not as nice a neighborhood as he lives in now," Suzie said to her father. Sir Julius looked about and felt that these cats were not good enough for him. Suzie introduced him to a lovely dark cat but Sir Julius put up his nose at his color and walked arrogantly away.

Suzie and her father took Sir Julius home. It was just no use. "I guess there is nothing we can do to change him. He's always going to be stuck-up. Dr. Tweedle can't help him either." Suzie sat down and cried.

That is the way it was for the next few months. Then one morning she met Mrs. Quiggly, who was running breathlessly toward her down the street. "Look at Sir Julius, Suzie. I saw him smile at me when I passed your house. He's changed!"

Suzie raced toward her house. She looked at Sir Julius. Mrs. Quiggly was right! He was actually smiling. She had never seen Sir Julius smile, or any cat for that matter. He was sitting in her old garage and beside him was a lovely grey cat and a litter of four kittens all looking like Sir Julius. They were all getting milk from the mother. Sir Julius had become a father!

From that day on Sir Julius changed. He smiled quite often and when he went to visit Mrs. Quiggly, she found him very pleasant.

"Being a father has certainly changed him. Wonder of wonders, I would never had believed it looking at him. I thought

FIGURE 13-2

he was too arrogant for all this. I guess he was just lonely and I didn't understand him. I'll even take one of the kittens to raise as my own, if Sir Julius won't mind."

"That will be fine" said Suzie, "I'll take the other three."

The three kittens that Suzie took were very friendly, but the one kitten that Mrs. Quiggly raised turned out to be very arrogant and grew up on her porch making Mrs. Quiggly very nervous.*

How To Make a Film from a Story

Several children particularly talented in art drew the illustrations on transparencies, such as that of Mrs. Quiggly in Figure 13-2.

---

*This story was actually read and illustrated on transparencies which were projected on a screen in a number of classes in a school.

For Classroom Use

Materials Needed

a. Acetates
b. Colored magic markers
c. Slide projector
d. Screen or reasonable facsimile

Procedure

The outline for the drawings may be made with white pencil directly upon the acetates and then gone over with the colored pens. The lines must be sharp for projection.

Each acetate is keyed to the story so that when the story is narrated, the appropriate acetate is slipped onto the projector.

For Assembly Use

The children of class 5-5 put the story of Julius on a tape. Mrs. Teller encouraged the potential actors of the class to read the words of the different characters. Merle did a shrill nasal Mrs. Quiggly, and Alan did a jovial Dr. Tweedle, and Suzie played herself. Thomas introduced the story and narrated the rest. The recording was played in the assembly accompanied by the appropriate acetates projected onto a screen.

Mrs. Teller's influence was there throughout the writing, illustrations, and production. She motivated, suggested possible dialogue and guided them in the illustrations. She also helped the children obtain the necessary art materials, the tape recorder and acquisition of time for the assembly performance.

The writing of the story opened the door for the enlargement of vocabulary: new words like arrogant, dignified, knight, invisible, coaxed, breathlessly, veterinarian, disposition and plays on words like "chip on his shoulder" were added to the class's vocabulary.

The teacher helped the class explore ideas, develop plot, and give free reign to the imagination in an accepting atmosphere. But she was there to, above all, provide enthusiasm for the multi-media presentation of the story, writing, art, dramatics, recording, and film-making.

The Creatively Gifted Child: A Problem

The creatively talented child is probably the most misunderstood and neglected child in the elementary school. We can measure the scholastically gifted child's performance and assess the academically slow but in the elementary school there are few valid tests for identifying the creatively gifted. He frequently is squelched or cast aside as an oddball in the classroom.

All children are creative. The creatively gifted child posesses these qualities in super-abundance. "They express such thinking in verbal, mathematical, scientific, artistic, musical, or dramatic media, in the dance, or in problem-solving in human interaction. ...These children prefer a learning style other than the traditional academic emphasis on knowledge, logical reasoning, and judgement."[3]

The relationship of the creative child with his teacher often determines his growth. A small boy becomes a problem in a fourth-year classroom because he is different. When everyone writes what he is told, he questions. "Now Johnny, do what I tell you," the well-meaning teacher admonishes. But he can't. His mind strays to other things. He begins to draw bridges on a paper and wonders how they are kept together, so he devises a plan for their construction. It is remarkably accurate but the teacher never sees it. "Stop that doodling," she calls impatiently. "I'm very glad I'll be seeing your mother soon." On Open School Night she had this to say to an alarmed parent. "Well, Johnny, he's something different from the others. I don't want to worry you, but I guess you might call him a daydreamer. He's always fooling with something at the science table when he should be doing his work, or doodling on paper, or constantly asking me those endless questions, instead of doing what he's supposed to do. It's really a lack of respect toward me as a teacher, maybe trying to find out what I don't know. Then he likes to get the others to ask all kinds of questions so that our work will be interrupted. Does he always talk like this at home? He doesn't pay attention to what I give

---

[3] Catherine B. Bruch, E. Paul Torrance, "Reaching The Creatively Gifted", *National Elementary Principal*, (National Association of Elementary School Principals, Washington, D.C., Number 5, Feb. 1972), p. 69.

him, always figuring out something else! Don't worry — with a little help, he'll probably outgrow it — we hope!"

The tragedy of Johnny is that he and Mrs. Louis, his teacher, are operating on different wavelengths. Mrs. Louis doesn't understand that he is a highly creative child, an original thinker who must have outlets; a boy who, if she might have looked at him more closely, has a longer attention span than any of the others in the class; a boy who probes for answers and meaning in the work that is being spoon-fed by the teacher; a boy who tries to discuss and find solutions in a classroom which does not allow for critical thinking and problem-solving. This is a classroom in which the very essence of any creative endeavor is looked upon as odd, disruptive, and a general nuisance.

What Does Johnny Need?

Johnny undoubtedly needs a different classroom climate; a climate open to his probing mind, a climate accepting his endless questions. He needs a creative teacher to set the tone for a classroom in which critical thinking can be promoted. It should be a classroom in which the intellectually gifted child as well as the creatively gifted child may express his thoughts without fear of reproval; a classroom in which the other children listen to him and in turn express their own opinions, and ask their own questions.

Critical Thinking

Let's take one aspect of the creative classroom, the encouragement of critical thinking. We assume that Johnny enters this room with all the facilities for critical judgment, but in reality he is just groping. He needs to be taught how to think critically. He must be taught to assess a problem, observe, collect data, see relationships, use judgments, question outcomes, and come to conclusions. He can then evaluate the results of these experiences.

Questioning can challenge the child. Provocative questions such as, "How do you know?" will help to motivate him to search for solutions to problems.

Open-end type questions provide opportunities for creative thinking. A list of open-ended questions for Johnny in science might be:

If there was no law of gravity, where would we be?

What if we had the power to heal all the sick?

Suppose there is no death?

What if there is life on Mars?

What if the sun loses heat?

These questions differ from the purely factual type which teachers are accustomed to dealing with. The open-end question has no clearly defined answer, and the child must supply his own from a pre-existing body of information. Children should be encouraged to formulate their own thought-provoking questions.

Brainstorming is another technique for developing critical thinking:

a. Start by defining the problem.

   A problem presented by the children might be —
      difficulty in completeing the math assignment.

   A problem brought out by the teacher might be —
      misbehavior of children in the lunchroom.

b. Invite the children to throw out ideas.

c. Discuss all the ramifications of the ideas collected.

Evaluating critical thinking is not simple. A checklist here may be used to assess the strides the children have made:

1. Can they recognize the existence of a problem?

2. Can they state the problem clearly and succinctly?

3. Can they follow specific logical steps in the solution of a problem?

4. Do they know and consult all sources for procuring basic information about a specific problem?

5. Do they inquire into significant reasons for actions and events?

6. Can they ask and answer interpretive and inferential questions? [4]

The tragedy of Johnny is perpetuated throughout the elementary school. He poses a threat to possibly drab teachers and this is unforgiveable. The fact is that a creative child needs a creative teacher who does not feel shaken by his divergency and independent thinking. Some teachers are definitely not suited for this kind of child. He needs an accepting teacher who is open to

---

[4] Adapted from Board of Education, *Guiding the Gifted* (Division of Elementary Schools, Board of Education, City of New York) 6, No. 1, June, 1965, p. 162.

ideas, assists in helping the child probe into new areas and is
enthusiastic instead of stultifying.

"Many creative individuals need guidance in achieving the
balance between creativity and conformity so that they enhance
one another. This is a guidance task for teachers and counselors at
all levels of education, because the creative personality does not
emerge suddenly and dramatically. It must be nurtured through
many crises from kindergarten and through graduate school."[5]

Summary

uidance through the creative process is a way of reaching
children. The disruptive classroom is often suffering in the throes
of boredom. Creative teaching springs from the interests of the
children themselves and is unafraid to explore new areas of
interest; this sparks the children's enthusiasm.

In class 5-5, one reads of a creative teacher who adapted the
situation which actually arose in a child's life, that of Suzie and
her cat, into a creative experience which involved story writing,
art, dramatics, and film-making.

The creatively gifted child can present a unique problem in
an average class if his needs are not met. The teacher must provide
the type of atmosphere which will allow him to develop.

[5]E. Paul Torrance, *Guiding Creative Talent* (Englewood Cliffs, New Jersey:
Prentice-Hall, Inc., 1962), pp. 142-143.

Chapter Fourteen

Dealing With Records
and Confidentiality

Children's records are a framework upon which the teacher can build. Although records in themselves are not adequate in painting a total picture of the child's performance, they provide significant clues to a child's personality.

Let's follow the endless chore of record-keeping of teachers in terms of the cumulative record card, recording of significant guidance data such as the anecdotal record, and the referral process or the guidance ladder of referral. Let's consider, finally, the implications of the matter of confidentiality and how it relates to teachers.

Guidance Implications

If one glances into a teacher's room at the end of the year, one sees her busy with filling in attendance data, completing cumulative record folders for each child, making out promotion lists, collecting anecdotal data for the child's records, filling in report cards and marking of test papers. Is it any wonder that teachers view any additional clerical task as a distinct burden? Yet it is the teacher who is in the most strategic position to provide the most accurate information in assessing a youngster, and it is the teacher who wields a tremendous influence on the youngster's future by her ratings.

The guidance implications of a record card are enormous. A record of a child, accurate or inaccurate, is only a glimpse into the nature of the child, but it colors the next teacher's thinking immeasurably. This chain of influence formed through the record card goes on from teacher to teacher. An inaccuracy in judgment can perpetuate itself when an inexperienced teacher takes for gospel the perceptions of more experienced colleagues. And sometimes a teacher can possibly have an influence in modifying a downward trend by giving an encouraging grade.

Timothy was marked unsatisfactory in social behavior until in the fourth grade one enterprising teacher gave him a good rating. His fifth and sixth year teachers rated him similarly. One wonders what subtle influence the previous opinions of teachers have on the ratings of children? How do these ratings raise or lower future teacher expectations of the child?

The Cumulative Record Card

What we're going to discuss here are certain aspects of the cumulative record card as it pertains to the recording of guidance data. It is here that comments should be added that will truly benefit the child's emotional and social growth. Record cards may vary from district to district but the following data is generally included:

Personal-Social Behavior

It is here that the interplay of child, teacher, and environment comes through. Teachers' estimates of social behavior are subjective. What one teacher considers a minor infraction of the rules, another deems a major catastrophe. Unfortunately, this is a weakness of most rating systems.

Confidential File

If there is a confidential file the teacher indicates this on the Cumulative Record Card. If a counselor is in the school it is generally kept in the counselor's office. If the guidance services are limited, the records are generally kept in the principal's office.

About Agencies and Special Reports

Teachers are not always fully aware of the agencies working with the child and his family. When a special guidance report reaches the school, it is generally directed to the counselor. The date and listing for a psychological report coming from a child guidance agency should be noted on the record card in the appropriate place, with additional information of where the report is kept.

With the hugh caseloads of counselors, there may be a breakdown in communication between counselor and teacher in the transference of this information.

Outstanding Abilities and Disabilities

What type of special planning is indicated for the child in view of his special abilities? Does he need a particular remedial program for his weaknesses? These facts must be considered.

Interests

Does the child belong to special clubs or is he engaged in other extracurricular activities? A record card indicating these interests will provide his next teacher with a tool for reaching the youngster. This is particularly vital in the case of a student who is not performing well academically. It may be solely through these special interests that the teacher can reach him.

Significant Interviews

Many record cards have a place to record significant interviews. If a parent or agency worker has been seen by a teacher or counselor, such an interview should be recorded on the record card as soon as possible (e.g., Conference with Mr. Harrold, social worker, Catholic Charities — Mr. Sorley, teacher. Summary in confidential folder). This presents a continuing picture of patterns of parental cooperation and agency assistance.

Remember the Following

DO

1. *Use* the record card at meetings as a base for planning.
2. Be *objective* in recording data.
3. Be *cognizant* that the child is taking this record card with him to the next class or school.
4. Be *positive* about the child. There must be some promising traits to indicate to the next teacher.
5. Be *thorough* in recording of special abilities or interests.

AVOID

1. *Using* the record card as a cathartic release about the child. Items

like "He is a nasty and ill-behaved boy" should be avoided.

2. *Diagnosing*. Many record cards have been embroidered with pyschological diagnoses of children which frequently have not been substantiated. Words like "retarded" and "brain-injured" should not be used unless entered in connection with special class placement.

3. *Divulging* contents of psychological evaluations on record cards. This is highly confidential information which should be kept in guidance folders.

The Child's Anecdotal Report

In order to ascertain patterns in a child's behavior from day to day, it is important for a teacher to keep a continuous account of the child in an anecdotal form. A simple anecdotal form for teachers to use is the one which lists child's name and class, teacher, date, activity, incident, and comments. This is shown in Figure 14-1 and is usually provided by the counselor. If there is no counselor in your school, you can prepare this form yourself.

You need not keep anecdotals for all your children. It would be impossible to do all this recording in class time. Just keep notations on those children who are potential guidance problems. In guidance cases, anecdotals should possibly be made out in duplicate, a carbon going to the counselor, so that she has a written summary of the child's recent behavior before her. This is urgent when the counselor communicates with social work agencies. Frequently a breakdown in communication between counselor and teacher may result in a gap in treatment of the youngster. The counselor usually retains this anecdotal material in a confidential folder.

And Remember!

(1) Be specific. Statements like "Lori is misbehaving today" are too general. Indicate the kind of behavior she exhibited, as "pushing a child in the wardrobe."

(2) Be objective. "Eric is a liar and really crazy" should be replaced with, "He did not tell the truth today about taking John's book."

(3) Record positive behavior. If a child shows improvement in a certain activity, state it, and possibly add your own interpretation.

ANECDOTAL   RECORD

CHILD'S NAME *Mary Thomas*
TEACHER *Miss Glass* CLASS *4-3* ROOM *324* DATE OF BIRTH *4-24-62*

DATE	ACTIVITY	INCIDENT	COMMENTS
2-3	Reading	Mary kicked Jill while taking her seat in the reading group.	Always disruptive during the reading period.
2-4	Reading	Mary fell asleep during the reading period and then suddenly woke up and hit Billy for apparently no reason.	Will take her out of this reading group — probably too fast for her.

FIGURE 14-1

(4) Avoid unclear rambling statements of behavior. Record each type of behavior individually.

(5) Review the confidential record for patterns of behavior, need for redirection of student activities, and need for supportive therapy.

The Guidance Ladder of Referral

In elementary schools where there is a part-time or full-time counselor there must be a procedure for referring children to the guidance services. Commonly, the assistant principal or principal receives the referrals for individual guidance from the teachers. The supervisor then becomes the screening agent, weeding out "the wheat from the chaff." He tries to separate ordinary discipline problems from guidance problems, although frequently one is a manifestation of the other. He confers with the counselor and makes the final selection of guidance cases.

These referrals may also be made by school personnel other than teachers, such as the school nurse, speech teacher, or parents.

A referral form will be provided by the counselor for the teacher to fill out. It will include such items as name, class, address, schools attended, father's and mother's name, occupation and working hours, siblings, significant comments on family relationships, home conditions, reading level and math level including test scores, physical defects, special talents, abilities or interests, significant attendance data, reason for referral and attached recent anecdotal summaries. (It is small wonder that a teacher with a minor problem would hesitate to proceed with recording all this data.)

The counselor follows this with an interview and observation of the child, examination of record cards, interview with teacher and parent, and examination of any anecdotal materials included. She starts a confidential file for the child, entering this information. The guidance process begins — it is now the task of the teacher and counselor to *communicate* with one another.

A Matter of Confidentiality

In a teacher's room, one teacher speaks of Tom's father who is unemployed and drinks heavily, and of Janet's mother who has taken a lover; they compare notes on the different children of a family whose members are in various classes; these children are discussed, evaluated and generally relegated to the category of undesirable problems. One teacher whispers that a "psychological" just came for Timothy and it doesn't look so promising (she heard), and he is definitely borderline in intelligence (she thinks), and another weighs the possibility that Timothy will wind up in her class next year, brain-injured as (she thinks) he is. In the main office, two secretaries speak in whispers of a mother who just left the office, and of a child who is being taken out of a foster home.

What is confidentiality? Does it exist, and what are its implications? Information about families will leak out through communication among teachers and other personnel. It is inevitable. Because children pass from teacher to teacher, a certain body of common information about his family accompanies him. However, discretion about what should be divulged for the good of the child is left to the individual teacher.

There are schools in which there are no counselors, and the teacher assumes a full guidance role. It is particularly here where there is a need for protection of the information confided to her by parents and children. It is here where the sensitivity and judgment of the teacher comes into play, protecting the privacy of the family involved.

There are individuals who feel that true confidentiality of information in the school system cannot exist. Even when the teacher or parent confides information to the guidance counselor, it is not considered "privileged communication" under the law. Yet such confidential material confided to a doctor, dentist, nurse, registered psychologist, certified social worker, clergy and, of course, spouse is protected. Teachers or counselors can be cited for contempt by the courts for withholding information. There is a need for protection of school personnel in this area.

This is not to suggest that confidential material should not be revealed for fear of consequences. Much information relevant to the planning for the child should be shared by the teacher, counselor and supervisor. (There are restrictions in the matter of psychological and psychiatric reports.) However, caution and sensitivity must be exercised by the parties involved; information bandied indiscriminately about the school can do potential damage to the youngster's progress.

Summary

The guidance data on the cumulative record card provides a framework for helping the child. To present a complete picture, there should be adequate visits, records of significant interviews, and noting of abilities and interests. This recording should be done objectively and positively, with a view toward helping the next teacher plan for the child.

The teacher also provides written guidance data in the form of anecdotal records and referral guidance information. The counselor uses this information for the child's planning within the school, and in school-agency communication. She enters this information in a confidential guidance folder made out for each child.

Confidentiality is subject to much interpretation and remains a delicate area on the part of the teacher. The teacher's discretion determines the extent to which confidential information concerning a child's family is bandied about the school. In schools where there is no counselor, much confidential material is imparted to the teacher, as she plays a guidance role. It is here where she must exercise particular judgment.

Chapter Fifteen

"Renewal begins with the school system as a living organism which must either develop or atrophy. There is no steady state."[1]

New Trends: A Humanistic Approach

A teacher stands before a first-grade class and has the children speak about their feelings. The children are being guided into thinking about themselves and the impact of their relationships with other human beings. It is part of a new humanistic surge in education; a developing awareness in children and teachers of themselves and of the world about them; a probing into who and what they are, in gaining self-understanding and self-awareness; the understanding of teachers that the emotional development of the child has an impact on intellectual functioning. Humanism is an interdisciplinary development involving individuals from the fields of education, psychology, counseling, visual arts, the theater, etc.

Humanism is not a new concept. Someone once said that there is nothing new but we must continually revitalize those principles which we seek to retain. So it is with the humanistic approach to education. There have always been humanistic teachers; we remember them from our childhood. They were teachers interested in our emotional growth as total human beings. There is now a reorientation in order to provide the kind of classroom climate suitable for dealing with the emotional aspects of the child. Humanism, then, stresses individual and institutional self-renewal. It deals with concerns such as teacher alienation and children's self-development; it deals with the building of warmer·

---

[1] Dale Lake, "Sensitivity Training: Some Cautions and Hopes," *Educational Opportunitiy Forum* (Albany, N.Y.: The State Education Department) I, No. IV, Fall 1969, p.162.

relationships, both individually and in the schools. It encourages training in creative thinking, problem-solving, decision-making, and interpersonal sensitivity.

This chapter will concern itself with the self-development of children and developing awareness in interpersonal relationships by:

- Exploring feelings
- Developing self-awareness through a value system

It will deal with the problem of teacher alienation as symptomatic of a need for better human institutions; in this process self-renewal of the educational structure is necessary.

Humanistic Teaching Concerns

As the teacher you must meet the humanistic challenge in your classroom. You deal with the development of many concerns, such as:

1. Developing children's imagination
2. Exploring feelings
3. Overcoming problems of motivation and relevancy

Let's Consider Feelings

Let's look at one of these concerns, that of educating feelings. How can you deal with the subject of feelings in your classroom? Are other teachers in the country employing these methods? Are they becoming aware of the complexities of feelings upon classroom performance?

"In Cleveland there is a city-wide human relations program designed to get children talking about themselves and their feelings about the issues of the day.

"In a school in Washington, D.C. feelings have been made a part of the language arts curriculum with youngsters being encouraged to write about their emotional lives.

"And in a teachers college in New Jersey, prospective teachers express their feelings about each other in sensitivity training sessions."[2]

---

[2]Joyce S. Enterline, "Project Insight," *Grade Teacher* (Greenwich, Conn: Professional Magazines Inc., 88, No. 3, Nov. 1970), p. 32.

A Second-Grade Teacher Explores Feelings

Miss Harris stands before her second-grade class and introduces the subject of emotions with the following class discussion:

Miss Harris: We can feel many things in different ways. Let's see what our feelings are. Do you like to have people like you? Does that make you happy? Now look at me. (She screws up her face.) How does this face make you feel?

Susan: I feel bad when you look mean.

Miss Harris: What else do you feel?

Robert: I feel the desk. (He touches it.)

Miss Harris: Yes, those are feelings of touch and are very real.

(The class becomes very quiet and a bit confused.)

Miss Harris: Children, I'm talking about feelings which are inside of you. (She jumps up and down, smiling.)

William: You feel very happy because you are jumping up and down.

Miss Harris: Correct, William. (She shows the children a picture of a girl crying.) What do you think she feels?

Sharon: Very sad or she wouldn't be crying.

Miss Harris: Why do you think she's crying?

Amy: She's crying because her friend said bad things to her.

Richard: She's crying because her mother whupped her.

Terrie: She's crying because her teacher is mean to her.

Sharon: She's crying because her tummy hurts her.

Miss Harris: There are different reasons why she might be sad, the same as there are different reasons why you are sad. Sometimes the things we do make other people happy or sad. Children, what did we find out this morning?

William: That we have different feelings inside us, like being happy and sad.

Amy: And I think when we do something sometimes it can make another person sad.

Miss Harris: Then what we do affects other people?

Children: Yes.

William: If we are bad to other people then they sure feel bad.

Miss Harris will eventually elicit feelings and emotions such as sadness, happiness, loneliness, fear, respect, and kindness. For her second lesson she had planned to deal with sadness by telling a story about a lost dog. She appealed to the children's imagination by bringing to class a delightful looking pink stuffed animal in the shape of a small dog.

Miss Harris: Look what I have. Well, since I couldn't stuff a real dog into this bag (the children laugh) I thought you might pretend this is real. Would you like to touch it?

The animal is passed eagerly about the room. Children touched its softness. Several boys began to bark.

Miss Harris: How many of you have a pet? How do you feel about your dog, John?

John: I like him and I play with him.

Miss Harris: Then how would you feel if the dog were lost?

John: I'd feel very terrible.

Jill: I would cry if my cat got lost and I would keep looking for her.

Eric: My cat killed my bird and I had to bury it and my mother yelled at me for not watching them.

Miss Harris: How did you feel when your bird died?

Eric: I felt very bad and sad.

Miss Harris: Well, I have a story about a lost dog which I am going to read to you. It's about a boy named Juanito who comes from Puerto Rico.

Carlos: Like me teacher!

Miss Harris: Like you, but Juanito doesn't call out in class. Well, this boy named Juanito came to this country with a dog named Pepito who got lost. Now listen, children, to all the places Juanito goes to find his dog.

Miss Harris relates the story *My Dog is Lost*,[3] a delightful tale in which Juanito visits Chinatown, Little Italy, Park Avenue, and Harlem searching for his dog Pepito, which he finally finds. When Harlem is mentioned, one child raises his hand frantically, "My cousin lives there!" Of course the children are happy and relieved at the conclusion.

Miss Harris: How did you feel when the dog was lost?

William: very sad.

Others: Very sad.

Lisa: I cried.

Miss Harris: How do you think that Juanito felt when he lost the dog?

Barbara: He must have felt very bad because he was in a new country.

Miss Harris: How do you think you'd feel in a strange country?

Carlos: I'd feel funny, like nobody knows me.

---

[3]Ezra Jack Keats and Pat Cherr, *My Dog is Lost* (New York: Thomas Y. Crowell Co., 1960).

William: I'd be scared.

Miss Harris: How do you think we should act toward people who are in a strange place?

Carlos: Very friendly.

William: Nice.

Miss Harris: I want you to think about what Juanito learned about the children in his neighborhood when he searched for his dog.

The class then concluded the lesson with the song, "Oh Where Oh Where Has My Little Dog Gone."

Suggested Follow-Up Activities

(1) Making puppets of the characters in the story and reenacting the tale.

(2) The film "The Toymaker" may be shown, refer to suggested film list.

Introducing the Subject of Feelings

If you are introducing the subject of feelings to the classroom, you may motivate the children by:

a. Class discussion
b. Films (see human relations films in back of book)
c. Story telling
d. Poetry reading
e. Games such as "guess who" allow children to see themselves as others do. (Guess who is the one in the class who--)
f. Record listening
g. Sentence completion (see Chapter Nine)
h. Song
i. Puppetry

The children are becoming more aware of their feelings and what makes people react the way they do. If you are the teacher who is introducing humanistic lessons into your classroom, you may take a cue from Project Insight, a name for Cleveland's city-wide human relations program: "It's a free-wheeling program in which almost any teaching technique goes, providing it achieves

its purpose; to get youngsters to know (and talk about) themselves
and their relationship to other human beings."[4]

Developing Self-Awareness: A Value System

In humanistic education we attempt to deal with the
questions: Who am I? What am I? What is important to me? The
child asks these questions in the search for his identity, but he
must develop a critical sense in evaluating situations. In developing
this critical sense, the child begins to sift out those things that are
relevant for him and begins to establish a value system based upon
his own discrimination.

In a ghetto area, the concepts of relevancy and black
conciousness are inextricably tied in with the child's emotional
growth and hence learning. These two concepts were reflected in
the following responses to the question posed to a third-grade
class, "What was the most important thing that happened to you
today?"

"Gym."
"A man came to talk about drugs."
"We heard a story about Pedro in the library."
"Lunch."
"We are going to give a play."
"I love when we all make things."
"Everybody act nice today."
"Lunch."
"Dancing to the record."
"The story about the black boy."
"Breakfast in the school."
"The movie on drugs in the assembly."
"The black policeman who spoke to the class."
"Singing to the music."
"Gym."
"When John got beat up."
"I got a new reader."
"No homework."
"Lunch."

---

[4]Joyce C. Enterline, "Project Insight," *Grade Teacher*,88, No. 3, p.33.

About Relevancy

Relevancy is a concern of humanistic education. What is relevant to the children's lives in the foregoing list? A breakfast program, lunch, a black policeman, a film on drugs, a desire for order, a story about a black boy, the renewal of hope projected with a new reader, and instincts for song and dance are responses showing this concern.

The relevance for the child in these responses has even gone beyond the classroom to extend to the community in the figure of the black policeman and to aspects of the social scene such as drugs. The junkie is part of the social scene for the minority child.

Concerning Black Awareness

In the foregoing responses, a black child reacts positively toward another black child in a story and toward a black policeman in the community, the child aspiring in the second instance to a higher self-image. Yet the matter of color in the ghetto remains in subtle erosive attitudes toward self. In a school fracas, one child will shout deprecatingly to another, "You really black, John!" The oppression of blacks in this country converts itself here into self-hatred. Education in the elementary schools of the ghetto has attempted to deal with this through black studies of Africa to give the children identity, but the self-deprecating attitudes remain.

Humanistic education is attempting to meet this challenge. "We are currently engaged in the research and development of processes that will help Blacks unlearn and shed internalized negativisms of the ego and self, to relearn and affirm those attitudes and values that nurture positive self-growth, and to learn new ways of coping with the onslaughts of individual and institutional racism."[5]

Problem: Teacher Alienation

Teacher alienation is a symptom of a system fraught with problems of faulty interpersonal relationships.

---

[5]*Program Synopsis, The Center for Humanistic Education,* State University of New York at Albany, Glenmont, New York, January, 1972, p. 13.

There are schools in which teachers are very much isolated in their classrooms with little outside assistance. There are schools in which there is poor personal interaction between teaching personnel. There is a desperate need to reduce these feelings of alienation among teachers by discussion groups in which personal barriers are broken, and, possibly, by sensitivity and encounter sessions led by qualified leaders.

Teachers from several schools were interviewed by the author about their relationships with the staff. Only the negative responses indicating teacher alienation are recorded below:

Everyone is interested in herself, it used to be different.

I never saw a place where no one knows what anyone else is doing, and what's worse they don't seem to care!

We have three women on the grade who talk to each other. I am one of them, thank heavens! We really have nothing to do with the rest of the school.

I don't know and I don't care! I'm just happy if I'm left alone.

Don't worry, I'm learning to be like the rest of them! Every man — excuse me, woman for herself!

In my school everyone changes for the worse. It's a fact.

Self-Renewal

How does one humanize a school system which breeds attitudes of separateness, indifference, apathy, despair, distrust, and alienation? Who has the responsibility to affect change, the most difficult of all problems in the educational institution? In this self-renewal, students, teachers, administrators, counselors, psychologists, and other school personnel are involved.

What is renewal? "Renewal is a continuing process through which intentions are made clear; needs are sensed and diagnosed; good solutions are invented; available resources are introduced and evaluated, tested, and utilized."[6] In the school, a measure of the

---

[6] Dale Lake, "Sensitivity Training: Some Cautions and Hopes," *Educational Opportunity Forum* (Albany, N.Y.: The State Education Department) I, No. IV, Fall 1969, p. 161.

responsibility for affecting better interpersonal relationships certainly resides with the administrator. The administrator establishes an atmosphere of openness, trust, and warmth, and must be open to the teacher's needs.

Part of the problem of affecting this renewal may also be met by the sensitivity group acting as a catalyst for change. The sensitivity group in this instance does not solve educational problems such as overcrowded classrooms, but it is "a tool which helps persons face the ordeal of changing, a tool which can reduce the personal feelings of alienation, loss of self esteem."[7] Sensitivity groups can prepare the way for change.

Final Summation

What have we been talking about in this book? Certainly one of the prime aims of the book has been to provide a more humanistic approach to the classroom. We have encouraged closer interpersonal relationships among all the personnel dealing with the emotional needs of the child. We have introduced innovative programs such as the guidance-reading tutorial programs, class meetings, and behavior modification involving commitment and responsibility on the part of the children; we dealt with discussion groups for teachers, exploring feelings and attitudes, encouraged creative self-expression of children through the language arts, painting, and dramatic activities; and increased class problem-solving and the development of the skills of critical thinking. Finally we have highlighted creativity, the lifeblood of the system, which should be fostered by supervisors in their teachers and students, for without a creative approach toward exploration, self-renewal will never take place.

As part of this total process of renewal, making better human beings and better human institutions, an improved setting will have to be provided for the teacher, child, and administrator — an environment which is open, dynamic, and above all, humane.

---

[7] *Ibid* p. 159.

Films and Filmstrips

Teachers, administrators, and counselors should first consult with their school boards for a complete listing of films available without charge. The following is a list of films and filmstrips suitable for classroom and workshop (teachers' and parents') use. The film sources are listed below with a code for easy reference with the list of films following.

Code   *Name and Address*

Material may be rented or purchased from:

COR   Coronet Films
                       65 E. South Water Street
                       Chicago, Illionis 60601

McGH   McGraw-Hill Films
                       330 West 42 Street
                       New York, New York 10036

WSP   Warren Schloat Productions, Inc.
                       Pleasantville, New York 10570

Material may be obtained on free loan from:

ADL   Anti-Defamation League of B'nai B'rith
                       315 Lexington Avenue
                       New York, New York 10016

BAVI   Bureau of Audio-Visual Instruction
                       Board of Education of the City of New York
                       110 Livingston Street
                       Brooklyn, New York 11201

BEVG   Bureau of Educational and Vocational
                       Guidance Resource Center
                       Board of Education of the City of New York

110 Livingston Street
Brooklyn, New York 11201

CAN   Canadian Films
               Press and Information Office
               Canadian Counsulate General
               680 Fifth Avenue
               New York, New York 10019

NCCJ   National Conference of Christians and Jews
               43 West 57 Street
               New York, New York 10019

NYS   New York State Department of Mental Hygiene
               Film Library
               44 Holland Avenue
               Albany, New York 11208

Classroom Films

Brotherhood of Man   (BAVI, NCCJ)   10 min.
Film shows that mankind's future depends on brotherhood.Grade 6

Drugs -- Use or Abuse?   (BEVG)   10 min.
Provides the elementary student with basic information about
drugs. (Can also be used for workshops.)   Grades 4-6

Hand in Hand   (ADL)   90 min.
The story of a friendship between an eight-year-old Catholic boy
and a seven-year-old Jewish girl. (Also good for parent workshop.)
                                                                 Grades 4-6

I Wonder Why   (McGH)   6 min.
A film about a young black girl who wonders why some people
don't like her.   Grades 5-6

The House I Live In   (ADL, BAVI)   11 min.
Frank Sinatra sings and talks to children about discrimination.

                                                                 Grades 4-6

The King and the Lion   (NCCJ)   12 min.
Award winning film is based in part on the fable of Androcles and
the Lion. The film stresses the necessity of gentleness and
kindness.   Grades K-6

Our Angry Feelings (NYS)   10 min.
Describes the causes, results, and constructive ways of handling anger.
                                                               Grades K-3

Our Class Works Together (BAVI, COR)   11 min.
Working together is the best way of getting projects done. We learn the benefits of planning and solving problems together.   Grades K-3

People Are Different and Alike (Cor)   11 min.
Shows that it is easy to see differences in people but that they are basically alike.   Grades K-6

A Place of My Own (McGH)   11 min.
In her family's crowded apartment, Rosita finds one unused spot and makes a place of her own.   Grades 4-6

The Toymaker (BAVI, McGH, NCCJ, NYS)   15 min.
Differences in hand puppets lead to exploration of brotherhood.
                                                               Grades K-3

Skipper Learns a Lesson (BAVI, NCCJ)   10 min.
Youngsters will be able to apply the film's morals concerning human relations to their activities at play and in the classroom.   Grades K-6

Ways to Settle Disputes (BAVI, COR)   11 min.
The film shows the give and take in the settlement of disputes.
                                                               Grades K-6

What to Do About Upset Feelings (COR)   11 min.
Provides ways for youngsters to deal constructively with their upset feelings.   Grades K-3

Classroom Filmstrips

Ghettos of America Series   (NCCJ, WSP)   Grades 5-6
  Jerry Lives in Harlem
  Traces the ghetto life of a twelve-year-old boy in Harlem.
  Anthony Lives in Watts
  Based on the life of an eleven-year-old boy in Watts.

Exploring Moral Values by Dr. Louis E. Raths   (WSP)
A series of 15 filmstrips dramatizing moral issues. Consisting of *Prejudice, Honesty, Authority* and *Personal Values.*
                                                               Grades 3-6

The Black Rabbits and the White Rabbits   (WSP)
An allegory dealing with the problems of slaves and masters and racial prejudice. (May also be obtained as a 16mm motion picture.)
Grades 1-6

Wonderful World of Work Program   (BEVG)
Stimulates vocational awareness by relating activities in the child's experience with the world of work. Vocational development is portrayed from this base. Titles in the program are:

K-3 Series:	Wally, The Worker Watcher
	The Junior Home-Maker
	The Newspaper Boy
	Supermarket Workers
4-6 Series:	Gas and Oil Workers
	Distributive Occupations
	National Resources
	Technical and Industrial
	Health Services
	Electrical Workers
	Telephone Workers
	Office Occupations
	Personal Services
	Home Economics

Index